KU-261-789

REPUBLIC OF UZBEKISTAN

Flag

Emblem

Territory	447.4 km2
Population	27.6 mln.
Capital	Tashkent
Language	Uzbek – state
Dominant religion	Islam
Greenwich Mean Time	+5 hours
Electric power	220V AC, 50A
Internet International	standard nets of a double plug.uz
Telephone code	+998

Emblem of Tashkent (1909) Adopted in 21.04.1909. Emblem of Tashkent Adopted in 1997
Authors: artist: D. Umarbekov sculptor^ A. Sharipov. Metro of Tashkent.

INTRODUCTION TO UZBEKISTAN

We are delighted to welcome you to Discovery Uzbekistan. The urge to discover is one of the most thrilling and deeply embedded mindsets of mankind. Uzbekistan offers many exciting opportunities for people of all age brackets to explore and make their own discoveries. It is Uzbekistan's rich historical legacy, unspoiled dramatic natural landscapes, ancient monuments, its hospitable inhabitants of diverse ethnical origins and the process of change the country is going through, which make it an ideal destination for modern day "discoverers". Travelling through Uzbekistan is beyond a doubt an unforgettable experience.

The Silk Road was the ancient 'broadband' or information highway enabling trade between East and West for 2,000 years. The Uzbek cities of Samarkand, Bukhara and Khiva were major merchant stopping points, or caravanserais, along its route. The Silk Road also enabled the exchange of ideas, knowledge and invention, that led to the cultural enrichment of the many peoples along this invisible track; indeed, it has enabled Europe to lift itself out of the Dark Ages. The Great Silk Road has facilitated a tolerance and openness to cultural specificities, reflected in the lively mix of traditions that exist side by side in Uzbekistan today. Take for instance a wedding ceremony, where elements of ancient Zoroastrianism, which had its origin in the region, are fused with Islamic beliefs and also with modern day influences in seamless harmony. This heritage and cultural fusion is what makes Uzbekistan, now more than ever, a dream destination for the modern day explorer.

The legacy of discovery of this mysterious part of the world, once referred to as Turkestan, encompasses a long list of intrepid explorers who roamed the mountains, deserts and oasis of Central Asia, often at great risk to themselves. The cloak and dagger exploits of Englishmen Burnes and Burnaby, the grisly fate of Conolly and Stoddart at the hands of the Emir of Bukhara, the missions of Abbott and Shakespeare to free the Russian slaves of Khiva, all fired the imagination of the Victorians during the period of the Great Game. This political match, known as the Tournament of Shadows by the Russians, occurred when Tsarist Russia sought to expand its frontiers towards the jewel of India and when Britain tried to outmanoeuvre them by acquiring influence in Central Asia, Afghanistan and Persia. Even following the Bolshevik revolution, Bailey reported back from Tashkent in 1918 disguised so convincingly as an Austrian prisoner of war that he was even given a mandate by the Russian secret service, Cheka, to seek out and capture himself! These amazing tales and others are recounted in the enthralling works of Peter Hopkirk, among others, that inspire the imagination of many a visitor today.

Modern Uzbekistan faces challenges of economic and political transition just like every other country in the world. A proud people, independent only since 1991, Uzbeks of all ages are trying to carve their own unique identity and way of life post the fall of the Soviet Union. Taking both Asian and European cultural roots they are preserving the best of their traditions whilst engaging openly with the wider world. Here there is an authentic and original culture so far completely untouched by the creeping global colonization of western cultural imports led by McDonalds, Starbucks and Hollywood. It may not resist this encroaching "Californication" (borrowed from the Red Hot Chili Pepper's mega hit) of the Western world indefinitely; so we recommend that you don't delay your journey for too long and visit - you are guaranteed a great welcome and an unforgettable experience!

The storks – symbols of Peace, bring Happiness to people
Antory

THE MAP OF UZBEKISTAN

TASHKENT: A CITY TO DISCOVER

More regular international flights serve Tashkent than any other Central Asian city, though many arrive at ungodly hours of the morning or late at night. Unfortunately Tashkent airport is not exactly top of the list in terms of its user friendliness or the visual aspect of its facilities and the first-time visitor is not in for a positive first impression when entering the arrivals hall; better to brace yourself. The airport is about 6km (4 miles) south of the city centre and a taxi ride downtown should not cost more than a few dollars, but beware the sharks that are taxi drivers lying in wait for tired and unsuspecting visitor. If you can, book your taxi ride through your hotel. It will cost you a little more than the going rate, but you won't get ripped off.

Trains run from Moscow via Samara, across Kazakhstan to Tashkent, or via Urgench, Charjou, Bukhara and Samarkand to Tashkent. It takes about 56 hours to get from Moscow to Tashkent by train. Bringing your own vehicle into Uzbekistan is a logistical and administrative nightmare and probably not worth the effort.

For many travellers to Uzbekistan Tashkent is simply a necessary stopover en route to the dream destinations of Samarkand, Bukhara, and Khiva. However this historical city holds many treasures and rewards, and upon deeper exploration you will encounter some unexpected surprises.

First impressions are of a gritty Soviet style city (it was rebuilt by the Soviets after the devastating earthquake of 1966). Wide avenues and tree-lined streets, imposing buildings and large squares dominate the 'new' town while the old town retains its higgledy-piggledy charm; low adobe houses turned inwards on their shady courtyards, winding streets, and ancient mosques and medresses.

A good place to start any tour is the imposing statue of Amir Temur in the centre of town (built on the spot where previously statues of Kaufman, Lenin, Stalin, and Marx have all stood). Uzbekistan's Russian past lingers on in many different ways but the city's oriental roots can never be in any doubt.

The liveliest stretch in downtown Tashkent used to be the street known as "Broadway", leading off from Amir Temur's statue. It was a fun place, especially at weekends, to wander and drink in the atmosphere, and to browse the antiques and souvenirs. Karaoke stalls did good business, and portrait artists, trinket and antique sellers, and cafes all plied their trade. In 2006, by government order, the area was closed to prevent an uncontrolled spill of unsightly activity and replaced with luxury shops, but it is hoped that there might be some easing of the regulations which may bring back

what was once a thriving hub of Tashkent, so keep an eye out for its revival.

One thing you should not miss is the Tellya Sheikh Mosque in the old city, which houses a beautiful Islamic library, complete with painted ceilings and ancient manuscripts on display. Another highlight is the huge Osman Koran thought to be the world's oldest Koran and said to have been stained with the blood of Osman himself in 655.

For culture take your pick from the eleven theatres in Tashkent. The Navoi is the largest and puts on a rotating programme of Russian ballet and opera and Uzbek folk productions. You'll often find all the well known ballets and operas being put on for a very reasonable price, by Western standards. For modern productions try the Ilkhom Theatre off Navoi Street.

Museums are also plentiful. For Uzbek arts and crafts such as ceramics, tiles, wood carving, embroidery and metal ware, visit the State Fine Arts Museum. The cumbersomely named Museum of the History of the People of Uzbekistan, once dedicated solely to the life of Lenin, now houses archaeological treasures including a second Century complete Buddha figure. On the third floor you will find more recent historical information about the current president, Islam Karimov, and his vision for the country. The Applied Arts Museum is popular not only for its beautiful exhibits but also for its setting. Built in the 1930s by a Russian diplomat who developed a love for Uzbek architecture and design, its painted ceilings, verandas, cool stone courtyard and woodcarving create a peaceful haven in the middle of the city and the antique shops on the museum's premises offer excellent shopping.

Wappen von Taschkent (1909). Wurde am 21.04.1909 angenommen.

Das Wappen von Taschkent wurde 1997 angenommen. Autoren: Künstler D. Umarbekov Bildhauer A.Sharipov.

DISCOVERY GUIDES

Aqua park, Japanese Garden
Anton Kovalenko

The State Academic Grand Theater of Opera and Ballet named after Alisher Navoi

Zafar Khusanov

MADRASSA OF ABDULKASIM SHEIKH (16TH CENTURY)

The Madrassa of Abdulkasim Sheikh, built up in the 16th century, was initially a complex, which comprised of a mosque, bathhouse and madrassa. The place, where the complex is located, formerly called Yangi Mahalla, was one of the main public centres. Originally, the Abdulkasim Sheikh Madrassa was a single-storey building. In 1864 when it was rebuilt a second storey was added. One enters through a beautiful arched portal, flanked by arcades and two towers (guldasta). The square-shaped courtyard has a mosque and lecture rooms and is still bordered by the dormitory cells in which students lived. For a long time Abdulkasim Sheikh Madrassa was located in a back street, yet, recently it has acquired a new stately neighbour, the Parliament building. Contrasted by modern Central Asian architecture, the historical madrassa looks even more impressive.

KUKELDASH MADRASSA

The Madrassah Kukeldash is one of most significant architectural sights of the 16th century. The main entrance, 19.7m high, which is arranged as an imposing portal, leads to the courtyard that is bordered by two-storied hostels in the form of sections. Each section consists of a room and entrance niche - ayvana. Two or three students occupied each room. The towers (guldasta) at the corners served as muezzins (azanchi), from where believers used to be called for worship (namaz).

DZHUMA MOSQUE (THE MAIN FRIDAY MOSQUE)

The first edifice of the Dzhuma Mosque (the Main Friday Mosque) was built in 1451 at the expense of Sheikh Uboydullo Khodja Ahror (1404-1490).

The Main Friday Mosque was built on a hill and therefore highly visible even at a great distance.

The Mosque of Uboydullo Ahror was badly damaged by a devastating earthquake in 1868. Though it was rebuilt 20 years later, the subsequent Russian invasion and the Soviet era left the mosque crumbling and indeed, in 1997 the ruins were razed and a completely new Friday mosque erected.

SHEIKH HOVENDI AT-TAHUR (SHEIKHANTAUR)

was born at the end of the 13th century. He came from a family of Saints (Khodja), who were considered the offspring of Mohammed the prophet. The Sheikh died in all probability sometime between 1355 and 1360.

The mausoleum (mazar) of Sheikhantaur underwent constant architectural changes since it was erected in the 14th century. The name is derived from petrified coniferous trees, the Saur that lined the path and that are devoted to Alexander the Great, who is revered in the region as the ancient prophet Iskander, and is said to have once rested on the very grounds.

THE QALDIRGHOCHBIY MAUSOLEUM

Qaldirghochbiy Mausoleum is a burial vault with a pyramidal dome, which is an uncommon sight in Uzbekistan. Tole-biy (Qaldirghochbiy) is a legendary judge from the Duglat tribe, which once actually ruled Tashkent. The Mausoleum was erected in the first half of the 15th century. The yard and its decoration have, however, unfortunately deteriorated over time.

THE MAUSOLEUM OF UNUS-KHAN

The mausoleum of Unus-Khan is located close to the mausoleum of Sheihantaur. It is the one of the two monumental buildings constructed in the 15th century, which still can be seen today. Unus-Khan of Mogolistan (1415-1487) was one of Tashkent's rulers.

THE KHAST IMAM SQUARE

The Khast Imam Square and the Barak Khan Madrassa were founded in the 16th century by a descendent of Tamerlane and who ruled Tashkent during the Shaybanid dynasty. The ornate facade of the blue-tiled mosaic and Koranic inscription conceals a rose garden courtyard and 35 hujras (small chambers). Visitors have to obtain prior permission to view the interior as this is the administrative centre of the Mufti of Uzbekistan the head of the official Islamic religion in the

National Bank of Uzbekistan
Anton Kovalenko

Tashkent television tower, view to Japanese Garden and Tashkentland
Anton Kovalenko

republic. Directly opposite Barak Khan is the Tellya Sheikh Mosque first built in the same era and now employed as the city's main Friday Mosque. Male visitors may petition the imam for the chance to see its beautiful Islamic Library.

THE MADRASSA OF BARAKHAN

The Madrassa of Barakhan was formed in the 15th-16th centuries out of edifices, which had their origins at different points in time. The initial body was a mausoleum east of the actual complex. The second element was the two-cupola Mausoleum-Khanaka, of Tashkent's ruler Soyunidj Khan Shaybani, 1530. In the middle of the 16th century the complex was rearranged into a madrassa. The complex was named after the ruler of that time, Nauruz-Ahmed, nicknamed, Barakhan. The entrance portal to the Madrassa of Barakhan is not characteristical for Tashkent by way of its decoration. Its bay is topped with a vault "colab-cory"; the tympanum arches and pylons are decorated with carved bricks and various mosaics.

THE MAUSOLEUM OF KAFFOL SHOSHIY

The mausoleum was built in honour of Imam Abubakr ibn Ali ibn Ismail Al Kaffol al Shoshiy an Islamic scholar of the Shabanid period. The first burial vault has not passed the test of time. The actual mausoleum was built in 1542 by Gulyam Hussain, who was the Khan's architect. It is an asymmetrically domed portal mausoleum - khanaka. Khanakas were erected to give pilgrims from distant lands a shelter by providing them space in the many cells for that purpose, the hujras. Mausoleum sites also often included a mosque and an eating-room, called oshkhana, with a kitchen. There is a burial place (sagana) on small yard south of the main building. The mausoleum is built of baked bricks.

THE MAUSOLEUM OF SHEIKH ZAYNUDIN BOBO

Sheikh Zaynudin Bobo was a writer and an expoert of the Sufi order, known as Suhrawardiyya.

An accurate date of his birth is not known. Popul belief maintains that Sheikh Zaynudin died at th considerable age of 95. He was, arguably, a s of the founder of the Suhrawardiyya order, Di al-din Abu 'n-Najib as-Surawardi (1097-1168), w sent his son Sheikh Zaynuddin to Tashkent with t purpose of spreading the ideas of his order. Shei Zaynuddin was buried at the graveyard of Orif village beyond the Kukcha Gate (now within t Tashkent city limits). There is an underground c (chillakhona of the 12th century) to the mausoleu where Sheikh Zaynuddin conducted his 40-d meditations (chilla) and a chartak dating back to t 14th century. The mausoleum from the 16th centu was rebuilt at the end of 19th century.

THE MAUSOLEUMS OF ZANGIATA - SUFI

The mausoleums of Zangiata - Sufi, who w very popular in Tashkent, and of his wife Ambar B - were conceivably built by Tamerlane at the end the 14th century. The real name of Zangiata w Sheikh Ay-Khodja. The nickname Zangiata mea "black". He came from a family descended fro Hazret Arslan Bobo; and also was the fifth "muri of Sufi Khodja Ahmad Yassavi who is considered t spiritual forefather of all the Turkic tribes of Centr Asia.

The mausoleum complex consists of th following: the Namazgoh mosque (1870); a minar (1914-1915); the mausoleum of Zangiata; a courtya with living quarters - hujras (dating from the 18th 19th centuries); a cemetery with the mausoleum Ambar Bibi contained within.

STATE MUSEUM OF APPLIED ART

In the State museum of applied arts of Uzbekista there are more than 7,000 displays of traditional fo art, starting from the first half of the 19th centu until modern times. The museum collection represented by all regions of Uzbekistan, many which are recognized as centres of distinct tradition crafts. Among the exhibits you will find ceram glass and porcelain plates and dishes, sampl of hand-made and machine embroidery, nation

ɔrics and clothes, carpets, works of wood engraving,
rnished miniatures, jewellery and many other things.
ιe museum is renowned for its atmosphere and the
arm of its objects. It also hosts trade exhibitions
contemporary works of art created on the basis of
cal traditional techniques. This museum is a must for
sitors not only for its collection but for the building
elf, a model of architectural decorative arts from the
rly 20th century.

STATE MUSEUM OF ARTS

The collection in this museum consists of more
an 50,000 exhibits gathered in five sections –
corative folk art and fine arts of Uzbekistan, Russian
d Western European arts, and foreign Oriental arts.
corative folk art and applied art is represented by
eces that date back to the 1st century B.C. These are
scoveries made during excavations on the territory
Southern Uzbekistan – in Khalchayan castle,
rakhsha (Bukhara), and the settlement of Kuva
erghana Valley).

MUSEUM OF THE HISTORY OF THE TIMURIDS

Amir Temur was a statesman, military commander
d legislator. He was the founder of a great empire,
e borders of which reached from the Mediterranean
a up to the Great Wall of China, from the Caspian
a to the Persian Gulf.

The museum holds a collection of objects related
Amir Temur and the Temurids. Descendants of
nir Temur include the great scientists and ruler of
averannakhr, Mirzo Ulugbek, the ruler of Khorasan,
ıssein Baykara, a gifted poet and historian and the
under of the Moghul empire in India, Zakhiridiin
ukhammad Babur.

Archaeological, ethnographic and numismatic
jects, armament and armours as well as objects that
e linked to the history of Amir Temur's state, such as
e correspondence of Amir Temur and his descendants
ith European monarchs are displayed. Furthermore,
tful miniatures and copies of Amir Temur's portraits
at were painted by European artists also form part
the collection. Some of the originals are currently
ored in the National Library of France.

STATE MUSEUM OF HISTORY OF UZBEKISTAN

The history of Central Asia is enormously
complex and there is no better place to gain a
deeper understanding of this region and its many
civilizations than a visit to the State Museum of
History. Starting from the Stone Age, the visitor
is led through the subsequent establishment of
first states on the territory of Uzbekistan right up
to modern times. Many exhibits of the museum
are world-famous. Among them the large bronze
Saxon cauldron of the 5th and 6th centuries
B.C., decorated with animalistic shapes and
drawings, or the magnificent sculpture image of
Buddha of the 1st century A.D., which was found
in the Surkhandarya region. The museum has a
fine collection of ancient ceramics and textiles.
Besides a large set of ancient coins, the museum
own more than 250,000 exhibits.

THE TASHKENT RAILWAY MUSEUM

This unique museum of railway equipment
was opened on the 4th of August 1989 in honour
of the centennial of the Uzbek trunk railway and
it is one of the largest museums of its kind in the
world. Among the many interesting exhibits are
13 historical steam locomotives, approximately
20 diesel and electric locomotives, engines
and mechanisms built and maintained by local
engineers and technicians, all reasons why the
Tashkent museum was included in the World
Association of Technical Museums associated
with the railway.

The main attraction (for adults as much as
for children) is an opportunity to ride on a mini-
diesel TU 7-A locomotive with two carriages.

ALISHER NAVOI STATE ACADEMIC GRAND THEATRE

The impressive hall of the Alisher Navoi
State Academic Grand Theatre has 860 seats.
The repertoire of the theatre includes classical
plays and plays based on national Uzbek
history, traditions and dance culture. Tickets for

traditionally popular ballets, such as "Don Quixote", "Nutcracker", "Giselle", "Swan lake", "1000 and one nights", as well as tickets for premieres should be purchased in advance. Among the most popular operas are "the Barber of Seville", "Carmen", "Aida", and "The Magic flute". Operas are performed in Italian, Russian and Uzbek languages. The Alisher Navoi State Academic Grand Theatre is the only Grand theatre in Central and South-Eastern Asia. Its stage hosts concerts, tours of foreign performers, theatre festivals, recitals of leading soloists and various festive events. The theatre's ensemble participates in different international projects and contests, cooperates with embassies and diplomatic representatives of foreign countries accredited in Uzbekistan.

CENTRAL EXHIBITION HALL OF THE ACADEMY OF ART OF UZBEKISTAN

The exhibition square (2500m2) of the Hall is the biggest in the whole of Central Asia. It was opened in 1974. Its structure accommodates the state exhibition management office, the Art Hamroh and Manzara galleries. CEH closely cooperates with foreign embassies, cultural and scientific centres accredited in Uzbekistan.

It organizes conferences, symposiums, round tables on pressing issues of modern art, meetings and evenings with representatives from creative unions of composers, writers, theatre and cinema actors. It produces catalogues, brochures and invitations for exhibitions.

GALLERY OF FINE ARTS

A very rich collection of works of fine arts of Uzbekistan dating back from the beginning of the 20th century up to present day as well as a unique collection of numismatics of Central Asia are exhibited in the gallery, which was inaugurated in 2004.

The state-of-the-art gallery with 15 halls on 3,500m2 includes a lecture hall, a cinema, a library, a studio for master-classes and an art-studio in addition to a well equipped facility for conferences,

seminars, presentations, business-meetings a㎡ other events.

Zoo of Tashkent

The Tashkent Zoological park extends ov㎡ a territory of 22.7 hectares and with its open ㎡ landscaped cages makes for an interesting str㎡ The Aquarium features life sharks, tropical fish, a㎡ 2,141 specimens from rivers, lakes and the sev㎡ seas. The Zoo is proud to list its attractions with ㎡ species and 189 specimens of mammals, 74 bi㎡ species and their 472 specimens; 26 species and ㎡ specimens of reptiles and amphibians. Furthermo㎡ Tashkent Zoo has specialized in the reproduction birds of prey and achieved considerable success breeding white-headed griffons, black griffons a㎡ condors. The cultivation of rare and disappeari㎡ species is the zoo's main focus in cooperation w㎡ 46 zoos worldwide.

THE BOTANICAL GARDEN

The Botanical garden of the Uzbekist㎡ Academy of Sciences is the oldest botanical gard㎡ in Uzbekistan and exists since 1950. The enti㎡ area of the Botanical garden is 66 hectares and㎡ is situated in the north-eastern part of Tashker The so called Dendrarium area of the garden is ㎡ hectares and it consists of dendroflora of Easte㎡ Asia, Northern America, the Far East, Europe, t㎡ Crimea and the Caucasus. More than 4,500 tree㎡ bushes, shrubs, lianas, grassy and water plar㎡ can be admired in the Botanical garden.

CHORSU BAZAAR

If you want to see how a local market operate㎡ nothing is better than a wander through the Chor㎡ Bazaar, Tashkent's most famous farmer's mark㎡ At the southern edge of the old town you can tas㎡ delicious fruits, buy exotic spices, and also pick ㎡ freshly slaughtered livestock. The odd souvenir the form of Uzbek skull caps, chapan coats a㎡ knives are also available for purchase. It's a go㎡ place to practice bargaining using any Uzbek Russian language you may have learned.

METRO OF TASHKENT

TURKISTON

YUNUSOBOD

FAYZULLA KHODJAEV

HABIB ABDULLAYEV

BERUNI

BODOMZOR

TINCHLIK

CHORSU

BUYUK IPAK IYLI

GHOFUR GHULOM

MINOR

PAKHTAKOR

PUSHKIN

NAVOI

MUSTAKILLIK
MAIDONI

A.QADIRIY

KHAMID OLIMJON

BUNYODKOR

UZBEKISTON

YUNUS
RADJABIY

AMIR TEMUR
KHIEBONI

MILLIY BOG

KOSMONAVTLAR

MASHINASOZLAR

KHAMZA

MING URIK

OIBEK

CHKALOV

BOBUR

TOSHKENT

MIRZO ULUGBEK

TUKIMACHILLAR

CHILONZOR

USMON NOSIR

DJANUBIY

A.KHODJAEV

SOBIR RAKHIMOV

IPPODROM

CHASHTEPA

TURSUN-ZADE

SERGELI

EKHTIROM

	Chilonzor-Linie
	O'zbekiston-Linie
	Yunusobod-Linie
	Sirgali-Linie
	im Bau

MAP OF TASHKENT

MADRASAHS
1 Barakhon
2 Kukeldosh
3 Abdulqosim Eshon Mosques
4 Nomozgoh
5 Djami Temples and Churches
6 Svyato-Uspensky Cathedral
7 Polish Roman Catholic Church

MAUSOLEUMS
8 Kaffol Shoshi
9 Yunuskhon
10 Qaldirgochbiy
11 Shaykh Khovandi Tohur
12 Shaykh Zaynudin

MUSEUMS
13 State Museum of Applied Art
14 State Museum of Arts
15 Museum of History of Timurids
16 State of Museum of History of Uzbekistan
17 The Tashkent Railway Museum

THEATRES
18 Alisher Navoi Academic Grand Theatre
19 Russian Academy Drama Theatre of Uzbekistan

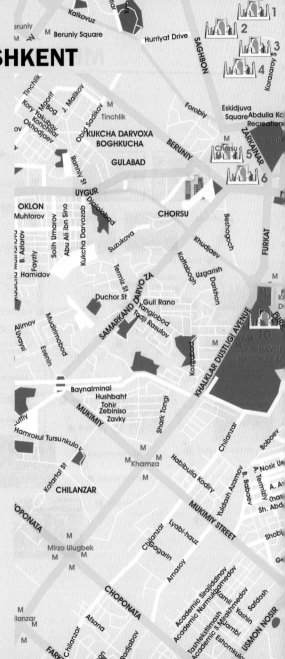

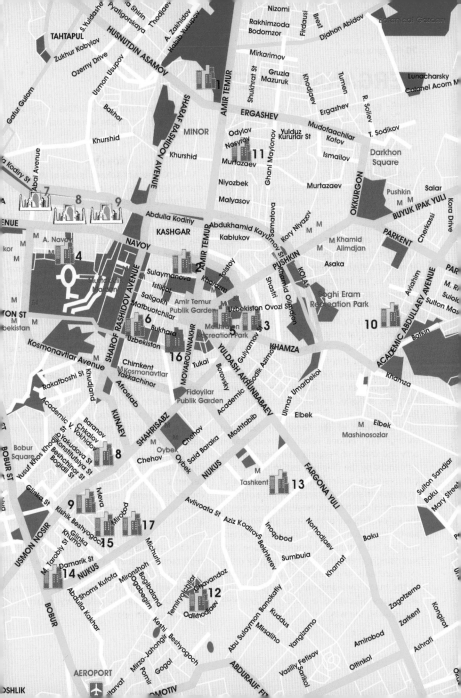

FERGANA VALLEY

The Fergana valley is a spacious cavity surrounded on three sides by the Tien-Shan and Pamir-Altay mountain systems, although when you enter the valley you will hardly feel you are in a valley at all, such is the vast expanse of the valley floor. Its length from West to East is 350 km with a width of 150 km. The Syrdarya, the second largest river of Central Asia, flows through the Fergana valley. Parallel to the Syrdarya, a manmade waterway, the Big Fergana Channel, leads water from the mountains to urban centres. Ancient Chinese sources claim that Fergana once was an independent state. The area seems to have been settled in the Stone Age. During the Bronze Age this particular land was inhabited by tribes who lived off cattle-breeding and farming. In 104 B.C.the Chinese ambassador Zhang Qian counted 70 big and small towns in this territory including Sokh, Uzgen, Kuva, and Akhsi. Among those that still prosper as small towns are Khudjand, Margilan, Kokand, Andijan, Namangan, and Rishtan.

One branch of the Great Silk Road led through the Fergana valley. For this reason arts and crafts of Fergana have been greatly influenced by the Chinese, Indian and Persian cultures since ancient times. The remains of architectural structures testify to the existence of Buddhist temples and Nestorian churches in the valley. This leg of the Great Silk Road was paved with stones to a considerable extent and had the status of a free-trade zone. Not surprisingly therefore, this was a busy route for merchants and caravans who made use of the many caravanserais, warehouses and workshops producing a variety of tradable goods along the way.

Numerous historical buildings in Kokand, Andijan and Namangan attract visitors from all over the world.

KOKAND

The Khanate of Kokand is one of the three states that existed on the territory of Central Asia before the revolution. In contrast to the Bukhara Emirate and the Khiva Khanate, which were Russian protectorates until the onset of the Soviet era, Kokand was conquered and abolished by Russian troops and joined to the Russian empire in 1876. At that period of time the Kokand Khanate was ruled by the khans of the Ming dynasty. Kokand was founded later than the other cities in the Fergana Valley. Nevertheless, soon it flourished and became an important trade and religious centre. The ruler's abode, the Khudoyarkhan Palace, is the most interesting building to visit, constructed at the end of the 19th century. It became the symbol of the entire valley.

The facade of the palace with four towers is inlayed with coloured ceramic tiles. The wide ramp leads to the main entrance; the gates of the palace are a masterpiece of wood engraving. The domed room of the darvozkhana is decorated with large stucco patterns. Khudoyarkhan's throne-room is the most splendid room in the palace. It is decorated with all forms of traditional applied arts; the ceiling is ornamented with 14 golden figured cavities, called khavzaks.

Khudoyarkhan's Palace is witness to all the important historic events that ever took place in Kokand. In 1876 the tsar's troops entered Kokand and occupied the palace. The khanate was abolished and the palace was quartered by a Russian garrison.

The bunch of grapes
Anton Kovalenko

The throne room became the Orthodox Church; boys and girls schools were established on the premises of the palace. After the October revolution, it became the administrative centre of the poor and farmers' union - "Koshchi". In 1924 the palace was the venue for the agricultural exhibition of the Fergana region, and a year later, in 1925 it was rearranged into the museum. During the Second World War it served as a military hospital.

MARGILAN

Margilan is one of the ancient cities of Fergana valley that long held the secret of silkworm breeding. The many mulberry trees along the way bear witness to this thriving industry. Up to the 14th century the town was a major stopover on the Silk Road. According to national legends the settlement's history can be traced back to the period of Alexander the Great. Margilan is the city of silk. It is famous for its distinctly patterned khan-atlas and its printed silk fabric. Via the Silk Road, parcels of silk from Margilan were carried on camel's backs to Baghdad, Kashgar, Khurasan, Egypt and Greece. With such a longstanding tradition it is not surprising that even today, Margilan is the centre of Uzbekistan's handwoven silk production, with a number of first rate workshops scattered around town. The Yodgorlik Silk Factory on Imam Zakhriddin street is the easiest to visit, open daily with its free tour and shop.

For nearly three centuries, from 1598 to 1876, Margilan belonged to the Khanate of Kokand. When Central Asia was integrated into the Russian Empire on the 8th September 1875, Margilan became the capital of the district and a wholesale market for silk and cotton. By then Margilan had seen numerous conquerors capturing the city. The Arabs, Tataro-mongolians, and Iranians left many a bloody trail throughout the reigns of the Temurids, Sheybanids and other rulers.

Considerable reconstruction of historical monumental architecture has taken place over the last decades. The complex around the Pir-Siddik mausoleum was constructed in the middle of the 18th century. Its name derives from the legend of a pigeon that saved the life of a saint. Pigeons are therefore now held in high esteem on the grounds of the complex.

The Khodja-Magiz mausoleum is from the early 18th century and is architecturally the most superior memorial building in Margilan.

A most harmonious composition – the Madrassa Said-Ahmadkhodja and its ornamental mosque in the adjacent yard represents the late 19th century.

Mosque Toron-bazar is from the same era and is a preferred site for it is a haven of peace for those in search of a rest in the shade provided by the old plane-trees.

RISHTAN

A mere 50 km from Fergana lies Rishtan, famous since the 9th century A.D. for its pottery. For over a thousand years, the masters impart their skills and knowledge of pottery work from generation to generation. Rishtan ceramics are shaped from local red clay, which is found in abundance around the settlement. Its specific glazing is obtained

Painstaking handmade of carpet weavers.
Afion, Zenjirbaff

by mixing ground minerals and ashes from specific plants found in the nearby mountains. The traditional big platters, the "lyagan", deep bowls "shokosa", water jars, milk jugs and many more vessels, ornamented with a glaze "ishkor" of turquoise and ultramarine colours have made Rishtani ceramic masters well-known all over the world. Ceramics from Rishtan are coveted gifts and prized possessions in both private and museum collections.

Just as Uzbekistan is the heart of Central Asia, the Fergana Valley is the heart of Uzbekistan. Over seven million people, about a third of the population, live in this fertile flood plain of the Syr Darya river. The main water artery sweeps down from the Pamirs into a valley approximately 300 km (190 miles) long and 170 km (105 miles) wide, surrounded by spurs of the Tian Shan - the Chatkal range to the north, Fergana to the east, and the Pamir-Alai to the south. It is the country's most industrial region as well as providing significant agricultural exports, including vast quantities of cotton, Uzbekistan's "white gold".

NAMANGAN

Archaeological excavations show that the city had citadel and strong fortifications by the name of Aksikent date back to the 10th century. Trade and crafts brought the city wealth and renown as Fergana's capital until the 13th century, whereupon it was razed to the ground by Mongolian conquerors and destroyed once again in the 18th century by a powerful earthquake. In 1875 Namangan became a part of the Russian Empire and was swiftly reinvented as a model Russian garrison town with the classic fan shaped street layout. At the beginning of the 20th century Namangan had grown into the second biggest city and the cotton processing centre for the entire Fergana valley, which had been turned into one of the cotton producing centres of the region. The Khodja Amin mausoleum and the Madrassa Mullo-Kirgiz bear witness to the time just before the Russian revolution.

KUVA

Kuva is one of the earliest settlements in the Fergana valley. The remains were traced back to the 3rd century B.C. During the excavations, archaeologists discovered the foundations of a Buddhist temple of the 6th to 8th centuries A.D. The first archaeological digs proved that Kuva was one of the leading centres of craftsmanship. It is possible that the art of glass-making could have originated from Kuva. Kuva is also the memorial complex of the famous medieval scientist Al-Fergany, who was well-known in Europe under the name Alfraganus.

Akhangaran reservoir
Mamadaliyev Sunnat

SAMARKAND

"We travel not for trafficking alone,
By hotter winds our fiery hearts are fanned.
For lust of knowing what should not be known
We take the Golden Road to Samarkand."
James Elroy Flecker 1913 – "The Golden Journey to Samarkand"

Samarkand has, since time immemorial, attracted people with its mystic's power. Throughout the course of history, the pearl of The Great Silk Road has held a particular appeal and an allure unlike any other city east of the Bosporus. Samarkand is legendary and the town itself has become a legend, not only for its turquoise cupolas but also its rising minarets, squares of hammered stones and ceilings decorated with gold. Past and present continue to mix on this crossroad.

The name of the town is mentioned as far back as the first thousand years B.C. in the Holy Book of Zoroaster, the "Avesta". In this book it is described as a developed agricultural region in the Zaravshan river valley where "the high mountains are abounding in pastures and water, providing the cattle with plentiful fodder, where deep lakes with vast water surface and navigable rivers with broad beds prevail..." In the Book, this region is called Sogd, and in the notes of Alexander the Great's biographer, Arian, a town by the name of Marakanda is referred to, which is situated in the present region of Samarkand. The city looks back on 3000 years of history. And what a moving history it has been, for Samarkand was one of the main thoroughfares of the Silk Road, a city where immense wealth was traded, a crossroads of the other Silk Road branches leading to Syria, Turkey, India, and China. It was under the Timurids, however, that Samarkand really came to its legendary fame.

Amir Temur had chosen Samarkand as the capital of his formidable empire that stretched from Kashmir to the Mediterranean Sea and from the Aral Sea to the Persian Gulf, aiming to build a capital to outshine all others by her greatness and beauty. From the territory he had conquered he brought back home the best masters, the greatest architects and builders of their time, experts in tile making, archery and armoury, master weavers, potters, glass-blowers, jewellers and many more. Conceived by Amir Temur and implemented by the hands of local and foreign masters the palaces of Gur-Emir, Bibi-Khanum and the Nekropolis of Shah I Zindah emerged as the monumental Islamic architecture of their time. The 21st century traveller is still awe struck before their grandeur and beauty.

Amir Temur's heir was his grandson Ulugbek, the great scientist, under whose rule the motto "The striving for knowledge is a must for each Moslem" prevailed. The main contribution of Ulugbek to the development of science is his madressa on the Registan square and his observatory, which had no equal at the time. Ulugbek determined an accurate atlas of the skies, listing over 1000 stars, the "Gurgan" tables, as well as a catalogue of geographical coordinates of many points on earth. Ulugbek's mentors were among the foremost scientists of his era and he himself as a leading scientist developed some of the great scientific talents, amongst whom Ali Kushchi should be cited here, who calculated "Pi" with an accuracy, which remained unsurpassed for 250 years.

Gur-Emir Mausoleum
www.kovalenko

The unique stand for Koran Osman
Melanie Everett

AFRASIAB

Afrasiab is the name of the legendary king of Turan. In turn, Turan is a name of an extensive territory, occupying almost all of Central Asia.

As the capital of Sogdiana, Afrasiab was conquered by Alexander the Great in 329 B.C. In the beginning of the 8th century the site of Afrasiab was conquered by the Arabs and developed into a cultural center for the Islamic world. In 1220, Afrasiab was conquered and razed almost to the ground by the Mongols under Genghis Khan.

Still today on the hillside of Afrasiab, behind the Museum, archaeological excavations reveal the remains of the ancient city.

REGISTAN

In the 14th century the Registan became the central square of the new site, Samarkand. Registan in translation, means "sandy place", from where six main streets led towards the faraway places where the precious wares traded in Samarkand were further destined, namely Misr (Cairo), Dimishk (Damascus), Baghdad, Sultaniya, and Farish (Paris), names still held by Samarkand's suburbs today. The architectural ensemble of the Registan is considered pre-eminent in Central Asia and supreme among Islamic monumental architecture. The former market place Registan is today framed from three sides by the Ulugbek Madressa (1417-1420), Sherdor Madressa (1619-1636), and Tillya-Kari Madressa (1647-1660).

ULUGBEK MADRASSA

This institute of higher learning in its heyday admitted at least 100 students under its roof, taught in the way of Islam, science and languages by some of the best scholars of their time. Its dimensions are harmoniously combined with the sublime elegance of its tiled façade. The entrance gate to this 15th century masterpiece leads into an inner yard of four arches with two rows of hujras.

SHERDOR MADRESSA

The second madressa of the Registan w built under governor Yalangtush in 1619 to 16 with the aim of achieving perfect harmony wi a second building of such grand scale and at th same time abiding by Islamic law prohibiting tot symmetry in the form of "mirror reflection".

TILLYA-KARI MADRESSA

Governor Yangtush completed the Regist complex from 1646 to 1660 by bridging the g between the two Madressas with an architectu master piece 75m in height. The breathtakii interior done in the style of "kundalas" a aureate inscription forming the word Tillya-K complemented by suras from the Koran are tl highlights. The colour spectrum on the long faça picks up the hues of Sher Dor with bright yellc dominating the lavish sunbeams and intertwin flower motives.

GUR EMIR MAUSOLEUM

Another masterpiece of Islamic architectur the construction of which started in 1403 up the sudden death of Muhammad Sultan, the dire heir and beloved grandson of Tamerlane (Am Temur). Ulugbek completed the construction a it is during his reign that the mausoleum becan the family crypt of the Timurid dynasty. It is he that the remains of Amir Temur were supposec laid to rest. In 1941, precisely on 19th of June, t unsealing of Amir Temur's tomb took place, in spi of the stone carved warning on the sarcophagu casting a curse on those trying to break open tl sarcophagus by force. The inscription said litera that "the one who breaks the precept of Tem will be punished, and a terrible war will break o over the world". The scientists present in 19 reported that Tamerlane's embalmed body w badly preserved and that his remains consisted bones only. Judging from the skeleton, the m ng in the coffin was a tall person with a big head. ▪e shank was mutilated, and the dorsal deformed, ▪actly according to descriptions of Temur's ▪ment. And exactly as to prediction, a mere three ▪ys after the tomb was invaded, on 22nd June ▪41, German forces attacked the Soviet Union. ▪as this ominous curse come true or a mere ▪incidence? The dispute continues to this day.

BIBI-KHANUM MOSQUE

The construction of the mosque was undertaken 1399, after the victorious campaign of Temur in ▪dia and was completed in 1404, within five years. ▪ Temur's decree the mosque Bibi-Khanum had outshine everything he had seen elsewhere. In ▪w of the fact that he had the most skilled and ▪novative masters assembled in Samarkand, it ▪s seen as a realistic endeavour. Ulugbek later ▪ced a monumental marble Koran holder inside ▪e Mosque, which was moved to the centre of the ▪urtyard in 1875. The entrance to the yard is a ▪rtal, 50m high, flanked by two round minarets.

SHAH-I-ZINDA NEKROPOLIS

In the northern part of Samarkand, on the edge the Afrosiab hill site, among the vast ancient ▪aveyards, lies a narrow corridor lined with ▪merous mausoleums. The most famous being ▪e grave of Kussam, the son of Abbas, the cousin the Prophet Mohammed. The deep turquoise ▪d emerald green tiles that adorn almost every ▪çade and interior give a magical splendour that is ▪paralleled anywhere in the world.

Among the people, Kussam is known under the ▪me Shah-i-Zinda "The living king", who, according Samarkand's legends, passed away from this ▪rld while still alive. On the headstone of Kussam ▪e following sura from the Koran is written: "The ▪es, who are killed on the way to Allah, are not ▪nsidered as dead: no, they are alive..."

From the entrance at street level, 36 stairs lead up to an ante chamber, which gives way to the necropolis. Most of the mausoleums stem from the 14th and 15th century. The architectural ensemble of Shah-i-Zinda and its manifold glazed majolica patterns are renovated today and premiere examples of the finest composed mosaics.

OBSERVATORY OF MIRZO ULUGBEK

According to archaeological remains, it can be assumed that the observatory, built in 1429, once contained the largest sextant in the East. The most precise instruments of Ulugbek's time were employed to provide hitherto unknown data as to the movement of the stars. The height of the so called sextant of Fahri, situated in the trench, which today provides the main attraction to the site, and which was discovered by the local archaeologist V.L. Vyatkin in 1908, is 40m. A small museum provides further insight into the accomplishments of Ulugbek, such as a fragment of the famous "Gurgan Tables", the most encompassing catalogue of stars known until that time. If you take a shared taxi, marshrutka, from the centre you can enjoy a trip through Samarkand's suburbs that will give you a flavour of real Samarkand life away from the tourists.

MAUSOLEUM OF THE PROPHET DANIEL

Among the hills of Afrasiab, on the river-bank of the small rivulet Siebcha (a tributary of the Zerafshan river), there is a wondrous place, the aura of which is immediately apparent. Complete calm prevails here, even birds remain quiet. This is where the Mausoleum of Saint Daniel lies. Among scholars, there is still no agreement as to when and how the mausoleum of the biblical prophet Daniel appeared in Samarkand. It is a sacred site for three world religions: Islam, Judaism, and Christianity. This is a location for pilgrims from all over the world as well as local inhabitants in search of blessings.

Registan
Anton Kovalenkov

THE HISTORY OF SAMARKAND PAPER

It is acknowledged that in the 7th century Samarkand was the first location outside of China where paper was produced. Later, owing to the Arabs and the spreading of Islamic culture, the secret of paper making reached the West via Spain.

With the arrival of the Russians and thus industrialization and an administrative culture based on paper documents, hand crafted paper making became an extinct art and cheaper, mass produced pure white paper became widely available to respond to this ever growing demand.

Nowadays handmade paper is once again available in Samarkand, thanks to support by UNESCO and the relentless effort and passion of the "Meros" craftspeople association under the directorship of Zarif Muhtarov, the driving force behind the Samarkand paper revival. The paper mill can be visited and the Meros craftspeople will gladly give you an introduction into this ancient craft.

Tel: (+998 66) 233 32 27

THE MUSEUM OF HISTORY AND CULTURE OF UZBEKISTAN

The rich collection of exhibits encompasses thousands of years of history, reflecting the way of life and events of the greater Samarkand area. Among the exhibits the following are of particular interest to the visitor: the original coffin of Amir Temur, which was replaced after the unsealing of his tomb in 1941; a special edition of the Koran, written on palm leaves whose length surpass 1.5m; a collection of ancient Islamic manuscripts and twenty volumes of the Koran, dating back to the 6th century. The museum is located in the centre of the big Chorsu square next to the Registan and behind Sher Dor Madressa.

Tel: (+998 66) 235 38 96

THE MUSEUM OF THE ANTIQUE HISTORY OF SAMARKAND

On the grounds of ancient Afrasiab, this smaller museum provides an excellent insight into the era of Samarkand's predecessor city, with ossuaries, fragments of blades, knives, arrows, coins, ceramics, as well as delicate frescos depicting city life, unearthed during various archaeological expeditions in the hills of Afrasiab. Just behind the museum in an open field you will see the remains of the archaeological excavations of Afrasiab, although today you will more likely see farmers grazing sheep than archaeologists picking coins from the dust.

Tel: (+998 66) 235 53 36

THE MUSEUM OF LOCAL LORE OF THE SAMARKAND REGION

This is the museum takes the visitor to an entirely different and more recent era in the history of Samarkand. Housed in the palatial residence of the famous Jewish merchant Kalandarov, the exhibits depict life in the early 19th century with its many facets, from the "Flora and Fauna" section to "Interior of living quarters and workshops", enhanced by costumes, furniture, objects, photos and books. One should not miss the beautifully ornamented concert hall in the left wing of the building.

Sharaf Rashidov Street, not far from the museum of winemaking.

Tel: (+998 66) 233 03 52

THE MUSEUM OF WINEMAKING, ATTACHED TO THE WINERY NAMED AFTER KHOVRENKO

With Central Asia growing some of the best grapes of the world, wine making goes back to pre-Islamic times, possibly to the Bronze age. The wines produced here have been awarded international diplomas and medals. Wine tasting and a shop are available to the interested visitor.

Situated near school №37, in Mahmud Koshgariy Street. Tel: (+998 66) 2 33 05 70

BAZAARS OF SAMARKAND

To witness the true essence of Central Asia, we recommend you visit the famous Bazaar of Samarkand, the Siabian or "old town" bazaar next to the Bibi Khanum mosque. There you will find the true hustle and bustle that makes Central Asia so charming and unique. Local dress and the Uzbek and Tajik language prevail and trade is brisk along the stalls displaying a colourful multitude of goods. Anything that can be bought or sold is being bought and sold here. From spring to autumn heaps of the freshest and tastiest fruits and vegetables you are ever likely to encounter are artfully heaped in abundance. You have to see it to believe it and the rich flavours will convert anyone to organic food instantly. Seemingly, not much has changed here over the centuries and for the passing visitor a bazaar gives the most vivid snapshot of real Uzbek life.

Customary to the bazaar, haggling over the price is expected, not with the sole aim to make a benefit but for the pure joy of the back and forth exchange between seller and buyer. A seller who loves his trade could thus be offended if the goods were to be bought without a haggle, but likewise haggling to the last penny would not be appropriate.

If the Siabian Bazaar has not quenched your thirst for that bazaar feeling, catch a taxi further up from the Registan and drive out to Urgut on a Saturday to delve into the wholesale bazaar, quite the experience of a lifetime.

SAMARKAND BREAD "NON"

Upon approaching Samarkand from Tashkent, Uzbeks will stop at the famous bread bazaar for Samarkand bread. The round lipyoshka (still called by its Russian name) is treasured throughout Uzbekistan. The history of "non" dates back to ancient Sogd, the civilization blossoming in the first settlements after the transition from nomadic lifestyle to settled agriculture. "Non" is baked to this day in the tandir clay oven and takes 5-8 minutes to bake. There really is nothing more delicious than to bite into a piece of "non" fresh from the oven. In the past more than twenty types were baked with such diverse names as "chahsak", "tafton", "Taftoni du bez", "tarkoli", "pulotiy", "fatiri chap-chak", "zaboni gov", "sohta", "shirmoi sedona payvand", "obi holi", "salang", and others.

CHRISTIANITY AND CHRISTIAN TEMPLES IN SAMARKAND

The Sogdian culture was defined by tolerance and religious freedom. Thus, for instance, in Urgut (40 km from Samarkand), a Christian church, Zoroastrian temple (Jartepa), and Buddhist monastery existed together, side by side.

Thanks to the Sogdians, Christianity spread to the Fergana valley and further to what was known as Eastern Turkestan, right up to Mongolia, Kashmir, and Tibet. Sogdian scriptures have been deciphered as translations of the New Testament. Nowadays in Samarkand there are four functioning Orthodox churches, one cathedral of a Catholic parish and chapels of different Christian communities: The Cathedral of Saint Alexiy, metropolitan of Moscow (Bobir-Mirzo street, 70); the Temple of the Saint in honor of the great martyr Georgiy Victorious (Birlik street, 66); the Armenian Church of Saint Astvatsatsin (the Blessed Virgin) (Mahmud Koshgari street, 70); a Catholic parish under the proclamation of saint Iowan Krestitel (Mahmud Koshgari street).

INTERNATIONAL MUSIC FESTIVAL "SHARK TARONALARI"

Every two years, inside the Registan, the international music festival "Shark Taronalari" is held. Since its inception in 1997, when bands, musical ensembles and singers from 31 countries participated it has now become one of the greatest festivals not only in Central Asia, but in the world. 51 countries took part in the 5th festival in 2005. The 6th festival coincided with Samarkand's 2750 anniversary, in 2007.

Shah-i-Zinda
Anton Kovalenko

USEFUL INFORMATION

Samarkand can be reached by air or by rail. Samarkand International Airport offers flights to and from Tashkent, Kazan, Moscow, Saint-Petersburg, and Simferopol. The Express-train Registan runs from Friday to Sunday, the "Shark" express to Bukhara stops in Samarkand and alternatively overnight trains link Samarkand with Tashkent on a daily basis

If you prefer to travel by car, your hotel will arrange for a car. If time is not an issue, try the transport hub is on the outskirts of Tashkent at the final metro station Chilanzar, where drivers are on the lookout for passengers interested in a seats in their Nexia cars. Although hitch hiking is never entirely safe, this form is a very pleasing way to mix with the locals and get deeper under the skin as well as experience some pretty dramatic driving. Exercise sensible caution when choosing the vehicle and driver, but don't be put off using this very convenient and efficient form of transport.

The best time to visit Samarkand is during the spring and fall, as summer, especially from June to August is very hot.

More than 30 licensed hotels and B&B's offer their services, from international four star hotels to guest houses. Almost everyone is now linked to a booking site so making advance reservations has become the norm, although turning up on the day usually has few problems unless it is a popular hotel for tour groups.

Samarkand offers one of the best restaurant, café and bar scenes in the country.

The most common national dishes in Samarkand are: pilaw; shashlik from any sort of meat, samsa (small cakes with meat, baked in a special oven, tandir) with meat, potato, or pumpkin; shurpa (soup, cooked of big amount of fresh meat, potato, or, sometimes, pumpkin, cut into large pieces); lagman (thick spaghetti with meat or vegetable sauce); nuhad (Central Asian big peas, stewed with mutton); moshkichiri (a squash of mung bean, rice and meat); manti (big steamed raviolis).

During melon season, try the many differen varieties. It is advisable not to drink water for a hour after eating a melon, only tea. All drinkin water is to be boiled and ideally even your teet should be brushed with boiled or mineral water.

Souvenirs and gifts from Samarkand are widel available at sightseeing points, in your hotel, souvenir shops and stalls. Here too, negotiatin the price is common. Objects less than 50 year old do not require an export permit. If older, the books, paintings, embroidery, carpets and kilim items from silver, copper and other metals, stamp badges, collectibles, audio- and video recording archaeological, geological and other sample that fall under category objects of cultural valu will require an expertise and export certifica available at designated museums.

The majority of inhabitants of Samarkand spea three languages: Tajik, Uzbek, and Russian. Yo will be surprised though how often you will com across someone who knows English, Germar French or Japanese. The city has a long traditior dating back to Soviet times and the onset of tourisn in the 1970s, of receiving foreign travellers.

The majority of local people conside themselves as Muslims with absolute toleranc of Christianity and Judaism. It will be highl appreciated if you follow certain unwritten rule while visiting mausoleums and mosques: n smoking and consumption of alcoholic beverage on premises, a hushed tone and no loud laughte no speaking while others are praying, taking o your shoes at the entrance of a mosque whil ladies are requested to wear a scarf on their hea when entering a mosque and to wear somethin covering bare shoulders at the very least.

Samarkandians are genuinely interested i foreign visitors and easily engage in a conversation As with everywhere, be cautious about strolling of the main streets at night and while visiting nigh clubs off the beaten track, but otherwise feel fre to roam and explore more than just the city's mai tourist attractions. You will likely be pleasantl surprised by the reception and friends you wil make.

Traditional carving ornament
Frank Everett

Gur Emir Mausoleum
Anton Kovalenko

MAP OF SAMARKAND

1 Architectural Ensemble
Registan
2 Bibi-Khanum Mosque
3 Gur Emir Mausoleum
4 Ak-Saray Mausoleum
5 Rukhabad Mausoleum
6 Qoraboy Aksakal Mosque
7 Bibi-Khanum Mausoleum
8 Shah-i-Zinda ensemble
9 Khazret – Khizr Mosque
10 Mausoleum of the
Prophet Daniel
11 Abu Mansuv al-
Moturudly Mausoleum
12 Chorsu domed
crossroads
13 Khodja Nisbaddor
Mosque
14 Ishratkhana Mausoleum
15 Abdi Darun Mausoleum
& Mosque
16 Observatory of Ulugbek

SHAKHRISABSZ

Always an important stop on the path of the Great Silk Road that led south to the sea, Shakhrisabsz is today a popular one or two day trip from Samarkand or a detour on the way to Bukhara. Situated in a fertile plain, with the Hissar Mountain as a spectacular backdrop, Shakhrisabsz looks back over one thousand years of history.

Shakhrisabsz means "Green City" and indeed, as you look down from the mountain pass over the plains, "green" and "lush" are words that spring to mind. The drive there takes you through a wealth of orchards, fertile fields and vineyards.

The architectural landmarks of Shakhrisabsz are at least 500 years old with the famous Ak Saray Palace and the Jahangir Mausoleum built in the late 14th and early 15th centuries.

Among the most important historical monuments are the Shamsiddin Kilab Mazar, the Kok Gumbaz Grand Mosque, and the Gumbazi Saidan Mausoleum. They all date back to Timurid times, which is unsurprising as Shakhrisabz was Amir Temur's hometown, at one time overshadowing neighbouring Samarkand.

The local bazaar and the city's ancient bathhouse, both from the 15th century are also stopovers on the grand tour.

Shakhrisabsz is a traditional centre of folk art and is renowned for its distinctive embroidery style, a very complex flat stitch that covers the base fabric entirely. The embroidering ladies from Shakhrisabsz and their purses and pillows are famous not only throughout Uzbekistan, where they are a fixture at every craft fair; their embroidered waist coats are proudly worn in places as far away as Canada and Japan. The imposing Ak Sara the White Palace, was Tamerlan favourite and most ambitic undertaking in this his home tov As Clavijo, the Spanish envoy Samarkand, reported back in t early 15th century, it was a colos structure with a pool on its roof, unbelievable 40m above the grou Beautiful filigree-like blue, white a gold mosaics remain and it is aw inspiring to imagine the splendc and size of the original constructi

KOK GUMBAZ MOSQUE AND DORU TILOVAT

The mosque was built by U Bek near the original mausoleu of Sheikh Shamsuddin Kulal, teacl and spiritual mentor of Temur, a Temur's father Amir Taragay. T tombstone of the Sheikh is s to have curative effects and it decorated with opulent marl ornaments, The blue domed mosc was designed as a Friday Mosc and, like almost everything Ul Bek commissioned, the shape the inner dome was executed w incredible geometrical accura and complicated mathemati computations which resulted in outstanding acoustic effects. T Imam, upon your request, will rec a sura of the Koran and a pray which will not fail to touch yc heart, whatever your religion m be. These are holy sites famc throughout the entire Islamic worl

Kok Gumbaz Mosque

TERMEZ

The first settlement on the grounds of Termez go back to the Bactrian kingdom in the 4th century B.C. and it is assumed that the foundations were laid by troops of Alexander the Great, who had a tremendous cultural influence on the region. The ancient name of Termez, Tarmit, stems from the name of the Greek-Bactrian King Demetriy, who mounted a citadel here. It is by way of Termez that Buddhism was spread from India further north to China. The citadel was destroyed by the Mongols under Genghis Khan but on that same strategically vital spot, the Russians built a garrison town by the name of Termez in 1888. The town thus became an important hub for power supply, communication and transportation, a crossroads of sort for telegraph cables, railway tracks and the road south to the Arabian Sea or east to Afghanistan. Termez grew into a strategic military stronghold on the Amudarya river for the Russians in their Afghanistan campaign in the 1970s. Today the city is also a key transit point for good from Afghanistan, some legal and some not so legal.

For decades a "forbidden city", inaccessible to visitors, Termez is nowadays the administrative centre of the Surkhandaria region with important sightseeing points in and around town. The unique memorials of Old Termez had since centuries been of interest to historians and travellers alike. Termez is mentioned in scriptures by Chinese travellers of the 7th century as well as by the Arab geographer, Ibn Khordadbeh, the famous traveller Ibn Battuta, the great scientist Abu Beruniy, and later the Spanish ambassador Rui Gonzales de Clavijo and the Hungarian orientalist Hermann Vambery. Unknown Greek, Armenian, Persian, and more Chinese and Arabic sources mention the town as well as its most famous inhabitant, Hakim-al-Termizi, by his full name Abu Abdullah Muhammad bin Ali bin Hasan bin Bashir al-Hakim at Termizi. Born about 750 A.D. Al Termizi grew up in a family of scholars and intellectuals and became one of the most noted thinkers of his time. His graveside and mausoleum are a must visit for they also allow a glimps over the Amudarya river onto the deserted plains of Afghanistan.

To learn more about the history of the area, the Surkhandarya regional museum (A.Temur str 29a, tel +99876 2273017) is a good starting point, as is the Surkhandarya local history museum (Festival str, ph# +998762237684.

Sites to visit outside of town are the ancient capital of the Kushan empire of the 1st century B.C., Buddhist Dalverzintepa. You may even be lucky to observe a Japanese archaeological team and their Uzbek colleagues at work, unearthing yet another building with its objects of cultural value and daily use such as coins, statues, frescoes tools, combs and jewellery within this ancient fortified town and its large temple complex. When Dalverzintepa was first re-discovered, a treasure of 36kg of gold, silver and precious stones was unearthed and made international headlines amongst the archaeological community.

Kara-Tepe is a temple complex of the 2nd and 3rd century well worth visiting, as is the unique building of the forty virgins Kirk-Kiz and the ensemble of the mausoleums Sultan-Saodat from the 11th century, the Kokidor-Ata mausoleum of the 16th century, and the brilliant Jakurgar minaret built in 1109. At the time of writing Kara-Tepe was off limits to tourists as it is situated right on the Afghan border in a sensitive military zone and special permits are required to visit. You should try a well-connected travel agency or two to find the necessary permissions.

Termez is the city boasting the highest average temperatures in Uzbekistan: the winter is warm; the summer is long-lasting and hot. As a result visitors in summer may regret choosing a town with a lack of air conditioned hotels and restaurants.

Regular flights get you to Termez from Tashkent and Moscow or you may opt for long train ride from Tashkent via Samarkand. As Termez is accommodating the German airbase, which supplies Afghanistan, there are now numerous hotels in the city and a host of restaurants and cafes catering to European tastes.

Landscape

BUKHARA

Bukhara I Sharif, Bukhara the noble, as this legendary town is cal led, is a highlight on any journey through Central Asia. The atmospher of olden days still prevails is the old town, where most of the hotels an B&B's are located, just off the central pond, Lyabi Hauz. Travellers a well advised to plan to spend quite a few nights here in order to delv back in time and take in the many sites the city offers and of which w describe but a few here.

ARK CITADEL

The Ark Citadel (the residence of Bukhara's former sovereigns and a citadel) is the most ancient memorial of Bukhara, with foundations dating to the 3rd century B.C. The Ark contained an entire city, with the state chanceries lying side by side to the Emir's quarters and his harem. During the long course of its existence, the Ark was repeatedly damaged and destroyed, but always reconstructed by a new dynasty taking over, such as the 16th century Sheybanids, who shaped the Ark the way it looks today. The buildings you pass or enter on your visit to the Ark were all constructed between the 17th and 20th centuries.

THE POI KALYAN CATHEDRAL MOSQUE

The Cathedral Mosque of Bukhara was originally situated near the walls of Bukhara's Citadel but was badly damaged in 1067 during a civil war. The governor of Bukhara at the time, Arslan-Khan ordered the mosque to be re-built away from the citadel, adding a magnificent minaret, the likes of which had not been seen previously. As medieval chronicles tell us: "there was not anything of it kind, so workmanlike and beautifu ever made". What the travelle admires today is not the origina construction, which unexplicabl collapsed soon after its completion The minaret casting its long shadov over the square these days was bui in 1127, is 45.3m in height and has diameter of 9m. Access is gained ove a bridge-passage from the mosqu and the climb is well worth it for th view over the magnificent Bukhar oasis.

ULUGBEK MADRESSA

Built by Tamerlane's grandsor Ulugbek, the astronomer, it is th oldest madressa in Bukhara, sti active today, which encapsulate Bukhara's role as the holiest cit of Central Asia. Its classic outlin encompasses a rectangular buildin with courtyard and decorated fron portal, the "peshak". The entranc is bifurcated by crosscut corridor (mionkhona), at one end leading int a lecture room (derskhana) and at th other end leading into the mosque There was a library (kitabkhana situated on the second floor, abov the entrance.

Bukhara. Old city
Anton Kovalenko

LYABI HAUZ

The Lyabi Hauz is Bukhara's "central square" that spreads around a central pool with its madressas and café's shaded by mulberry trees. It has existed since the 1620s and means "around the pool" in the local Tajik based language. Although it has become undeniably touristy in recent years one can easily imagine skull-capped locals drinking tea and discussing business just a century or two ago.

EMIR'S SUMMER PALACE

4 kilometres away from Bukhara, along the road, leading to Guzhduvan from the Samarkand gates, a magnificent summer palace of the last Bukharian emir's dynasty, Sitorai Mokhi Khosa (the castle similar to the Star and Moon) dominates.

The first palace constructions were built in the period of Emir Nasrullokhan's government (1826-1860).

General constructions of the summer palace were erected in the governing years of Bukharian emir, Mirsaid Alimkhan (1911-1920). The palace divides into old one and new one. The new palace's official reception room resembles the shape of the letter "П". There is a high terrace, called the salomkhona (greeting-room) on its north side, with the ziyofatlar zali (living room), kutish zali (waiting hall), takhthona (throne room) and khazinakhona (treasury) on its north and east side of palace.

NODIR DEVON BEGI MADRESSA

The façade of this madressa, with its sun and semurg birds, and the impressive wooden gate is a true Bukharan landmark. The beautiful inner courtyard is the heart of Bukhara and offers a particularly enchanting atmosphere at all times of the day, with its charming crafts people and sellers. In the evening, a folklore show with life music and national dances interlaced with the well choreographed Fashion and Costume show is a highlight on the travel agenda. Dinner is served upon advance booking.

CHOR-MINOR MADRESSA

Not far from Lyabi Hauz, accessible through narrow lanes towards the northeastern part of town, a square opens to an extraordinary memorial of 17th century. Chor Minor, Four Minarets is a madressa commissioned in 1807 by the wealthy Turkmen Khalif Niyaz-Kula. It has not been entirely determined what role the madressa played. It was likely part of a larger complex serving a dual purpose, namely that of both a place of worship and habitat.

MAGOK-I-ATTORY MOSQUE

There was a bazaar here before the Arab conquest, where herbs, potions, and spices were traded and the goddess of the moon, Mokh, was worshipped in a Zoroastrian temple. Later on, the temple was replaced by a mosque. The first part of the name, "Magok" means "pit" or "excavated", because its entrance is halfway below the surface.

The revival of the repeatedly damaged mosque dates back to 1546 as indicated by an inscription above the portal and it has housed a Buddhist temple, a Zoroastrian temple and a jewish synagogue at points in its history prior to the 16th century.

MAUSOLEUM OF THE SAMANIDS

The Mausoleum, which is the family grave of the Samanid sovereign's dynasty, represents one of the premiere architectural samples of artful brickwork typical of the Samanid's governing period (875-999).

In a beautiful park, the perfect cube topped by a half-sphere dome stands all on its own. Its seemingly ever-changing appearance throughout the day is due to the shadow cast by the patterns shaped by the protruding bricks in ever new constellations. The mausoleum's intricacy is a photographer's dream subject.

CHASHMA-AYUB MAUSOLEUM (SPRING OF JOVE)

As one exits the park, one passes the Mausoleum of Chashma-Ayub (i.e. Spring of Jove), which has been restored to its former splendour. It is a building from the 14th century, shaped into an oblong prism and crowned with various domes above rooms of different size and shapes. Underneath a double dome lays the spring where pilgrims come to drink the sacred water.

The spring is linked to the legend of the Prophet Jove. During a drought, the local people, dying from thirst, appealed to Jove to send them water. When Jove, in response to the plea, stroked the ground with this baton, a salutary spring appeared from which fresh water streamed to the delight of the thirsty, and still does so today.

JEWISH QUARTERS

The Bukharian Jewish community today comprises of over 50 families. Their ancestors' contribution to arts, music, crafts, and textiles which made Bukhara at one time the mysterious and coveted destination of many tradesmen and adventurers cannot be over-estimated. A visit to the synagogue, the Jewish school and the soon-to-be-opened Jewish Museum will allow you a glimpse into the life of these modern and well-integrated citizens.

ARTS AND CRAFTS, ENTERTAINMENT

Bukhara is a shopper's paradise for souvenir's from Uzbekistan, doing its former reputation as a main trading point full justice. Of the five trading domes, three are still in operation. Under their cupolas, an amazing display of objects that have

Chor-Minor Madressa
Anton Kovalenko

shaped The Great Silk Road find eager buyers. Silk to spices, antiques to contemporary works of art and a very lively crafts scene make this an essential visit for anyone who wants to experience what ancient commerce would have felt like in the legend that was Bukhara. Arts and crafts are produced before your eyes in a number of Caravanserais by masters who have built themselves an international reputation. For instance visit those in the Artisan Development Centre inside the Caravanserai Saifiddin or the masters at the Caravanserai Nugai, where you are also given the opportunity to taste the finest wines from the region and learn from an expert. It is impossible not to find the perfect souvenir or gift in Bukhara, at any budget, from carpets to jewellery and textiles to ceramics. Or how about a string instrument? String instruments originated in Central Asia. Bukharian masters hand carve a variety of instruments, and are always happy to demonstrate their art or let you try out an instrument while telling you about the history and their love for their craft and for music.

One of the most widespread crafts of contemporary Bukhara is gold embroidery. Once only men practiced the art of stitching these delicate threads to velvet, but today gold embroidery is in the able hands of many women. No wedding, no celebration, no Sunday stroll with the family, no interior design would be imaginable without these distinctive metal stitched patterns. Choose from a wide range of clothing and accessories to take home as a souvenir.

There are two places in the world where carpets based on patterns found on original Timurid miniature paintings are being woven; one is Bukhara, the other Khiva, both thanks to a UNESCO initiative. The Bukhara workshop is located in the Eshoni Pir madressa. You can watch every stage, from the original design to the finished article.

Bukhara as seen through the lens of a local master photographer, some of whom have studied in the USA, gives you a whole new perspective. A visit to the Centre for the Development of Creative Photography is an eye opener. Travelling exhibitions and varying monthly themes give interesting new angles on Central Asia. The centre is located in the small gem of a madressa opposite the Art Gallery.

BUKHARA FOR THE LITTLE ONES

Bukhara with children? Why not? Some private hotels offer a babysitting service and there is plenty of interest for young visitors around the central hauz or pool and in the colourful trading domes. In the evenings visit the Puppet

Mausoleum of Samanids. Border of 19-20 centuries

Theatre, where short sequences from Bukharian legends and funny stories by Nasriddin Effendi are enacted in English. You can also visit the summer stage right by Lyabi Hauz, which is in operation daily when in season.

SATORI I MAGOKI SARAI

It seems unfortunate that the last Emir of Bukhara, Alim Khan, was not able to enjoy his Summer Palace for long. Commissioned in 1826 under Nasrullokhan and finished just before the revolution by Mirsaid Alim Khan, the Palace is a wonderful example of how the Bukharian Emirs adapted to new style trends from abroad, especially in their reception halls. Sitora I Mokhi Khoza and its surroundings are delightful and make an interesting contrast to the 16th century old town. Take your time exploring the splendidly decorated reception rooms, the harem, the textile museum in one of the pavilions, and wander down to the lake along shady avenues where proud peacocks strut.

PAYKENT

The forerunner of Bukhara and high culture city state, not ruled by a governor but a merchants' republic from the 2nd century, fell into abandon after multiple conquests and destructions and ultimately when the river, at which shores it was built, changed its course. The archaeological site and the museum of Paykent are a 45 minute drive from Lyabi Hauz, in the lower reaches of the Zerafshan river, and is a must for those with time on their hand or on a repeat visit. You will invariably run into visiting scholars on archaeological expeditions, often from the Hermitage in St. Petersburg, who can give you background information on this Sogdian city, which held a key position along The Great Silk Road.

WHERE TO STAY AND WHERE TO EAT

From boutique hotel to family guest house, Bukhara offers the widest range and most ample choice of accommodation. There is a perfect place to stay for everyone, every taste, preference and budget but it takes tenacity to find the hotel most suited to you. Private hoteliers are happy to open the gate to their B&Bs and show you a room. You will be stunned at the wonderful atmosphere and creativity behind closely shut gates. Remember that taxi drivers may not always be the best source of information for insider tips on what guests would consider the best place in town. Most cafes and restaurant are along Nakshbandi Street, leading from the airport all the way through the old town along Lyabi Hauz to the women's madressa. Always ask for home cooking at your hotel.

Poi Kalan
Anton Kovalenko

The general view of the city
Anton Kovalenko

MAP OF BUKHARA

1 Ark Fortress
2 Ark Museum
3 Ulugbek Madressa
4 Abdullazizkhan Madressa
5 Chor Minor Madressa
6 Kukeltash Madressa
7 Miri Arab Madressa
8 Nadir Divan Begi Madressa
9 Mullo Tirsunjan Madressa
10 Magok-i-Attory Mosque
11 Mausoleum of the Samanids
12 Lyabi Hauz
13 Khodja Zaynudin complex
14 The Poi Kayan Cathedral Mosque
15 Khammon Kunjak Mosque
16 Zindan (former prison)
17 Toki Zargaron Trading dome
18 Abdullah Khan Madressa
19 Toki Telpak Furushon Trading dome
20 Toki Sarrafon Trading dome
21 Goziyon Madressa
22 Zabiyon Davijon Mosque
23 Nodir Divanbegi Khanaka
24 Bolo-Khaus Mosque & Minaret
25 Modari Khan Madressa
26 Chashma Ayub Mausoleum

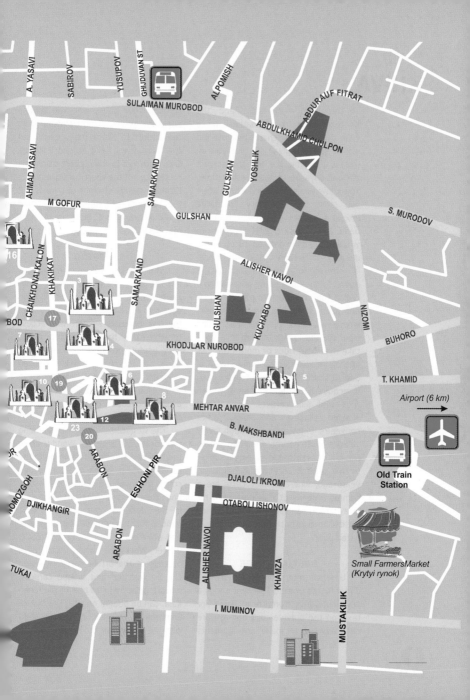

A. YASAVI

SABIROV

YUSUPOV

GHJDUVAN ST

SULAIMAN MUROBOD

ALPOMISH

ABDURAUF FITRAT

ABDULKHAMID CHULPON

S. MURODOV

AHMAD YASAVI

M GOFUR

SAMARKAND

GULSHAN

GULSHAN

YOSHLIK

ALISHER NAVOI

CHAIKHONAI KALON

KHAKIKAT

16

BOD

17

7

SAMARKAND

3

GULSHAN

KUCHABO

NIZOMI

BUHORO

KHODJLAR NUROBOD

4

10

19

6

5

T. KHAMID

Airport (6 km)

8

MEHTAR ANVAR

12

23

B. NAKSHBANDI

20

ARABON

ESHONI PIR

DJALOLI IKROMI

Old Train
Station

NOMOZGOH

DJIKHANGIR

OTABOLI ISHONOV

ARABON

ALISHER NAVOI

KHAMZA

Small FarmersMarket
(Krytyi rynok)

TUKAI

I. MUMINOV

MUSTAKILIK

KHIVA

The history of Khiva and the Khorezm oasis is fascinating and a walk through the Ichan Kala, the old walled city of Khiva, will give you an insight into the life led there from ancient days up to the present time. You know you are nearing Khiva when you cross the legendary Amudarya (Oxus) river. As you round the last bend, the mighty citadel rises before you and the main gate opens up to the old city. It becomes clear why Khiva is referred to as a museum in the open. Today Khiva is the gateway to a region that has much to offer: Ancient Khorezm, stretching up to Muynak, where you may discover lost cities from the 6th century, sleep in a yurt, take river boat rides or mourn the loss of a major water ecosystem in the Aral Sea. It's also the region in Uzbekistan to acquire handmade ceramics, woven rugs and silk carpets, embroidery, woollen slippers and many other souvenirs. Enjoy a drive through lovely villages made entirely from clay where friendly peasants lead a lifestyle similar to that of their ancestors hundreds of years ago, where donkey carts are a common means of transportation, far away from sophistication and fancy establishments but where hospitality is paramount.

GETTING THERE

Urgench International Airport has direct flights from to Tashkent and is a 40 minute drive from Khiva. There are taxis on the outside curb but you are best advised to make arrangements through your hotel, who will send a car with driver. The tramway from the airport to Khiva really exists but the journey will take around 2 hours. Overland from Tashkent there is only one route, no, not the short cut through the Kizilkum desert straight out west, but the 1000km road through Samarkand and Bukhara. A local bus from Bukhara may take up to 12 hours.

SHOPPING

What strikes you at first glance are the seas of thick, woollen, hand-knitted socks, which every lady in town seems to have on sale. Wool is one of the raw materials women have access to, which they have learnt to turn into very useful, practical and affordable items. By purchasing these woollen "slippers", you help the ladies in Khiva to provide for their family and enable a good education of their children. A cause well worth supporting.

The woodcarving in Khiva is among the finest in Uzbekistan. Wander down the narrow lanes and pass through the carved wooden gates into the hidden courtyards, where a number of masters and their apprentices are engaged in this detailed craft. Khiva is also famous for its ceramics and their blue and white glaze. Step into the UNESCO Carpet Workshop, where the entire process of the art of carpet weaving can be watched and unique carpets, mirroring the majolica tiles of the Ichan Kala, can be bought on site. The Suzani Embroidery Workshop, established with the support of the British Council, makes beautifully handcrafted gifts for yourself or to give to friends and family back home. At the Alla Kulli Khan Madressa, which was elaborately restored a few years back, you will find some interesting shops including handwoven Allacha (woven on site), the striped cloth of traditional Khorezm chapan coats. The turquoise Khiva ceramics are very specific to the area and cannot be bought elsewhere. Try to find antique ceramic plates in the shop behind the tourism information centre. Hand puppets are a specialty of the Khiva puppet masters and a wonderful way to recount your journey along the Silk Road to children back home.

HOTELS

Your top of the range options include the wonderful Malika Hotel, which lies just outside the city walls on the hauz or pond, reflecting its majolica tiled facade. Outside the western wall there is the brand new Marco Polo Asia Hotel. You can even stay inside the Ichan Kala walls, where you have the choice between the ever expanding Archanchi Hotel, Hotel Lola right in the centre, the lovely family-run Mirzobashi Guest House right opposite Katya, the camel's lair, the Mirzobashi Hotel, Hotel Islambek, Sheharazade B&B, Meros Guest House and Zafar Bek Hotel near the south-eastern gate.

CHAI KHANAS

There are several small tea houses to be found inside Ichan Kala; delicious manti and fried fish are found at the Zarafshan Chai Khana; ice cream specialties and cold drinks are available under the aywan just to the left of the main gate and tasty lunch and dinners can be had at Bir Gumbaz near the Information Centre. Chai Khana Farruh, on the main pedestrian zone, is a good alternative. With advance booking, wonderful home cooking can be enjoyed at Mirzobashi and in general every hotel is happy to serve lunch and dinner with some advance notice. Don't miss out on steaming plov from Khorezm and fish specialties prepared from the day's catch from the Amu Darya river.

Cool down in the heat of the summer with an ice cream, available on every corner, or try a cool local beer in the evening under the stars and believe us, the night sky as seen from the old town is something else and will imprint Khiva forever in your memory.

ICHAN-KALA

Ichan-Kala is the most densely populated part of Khiva, comprising both private residences and historic monuments turned into museums. Pass the Ichan-Kala from the main gate Darvaza all the way to the gate close to the bazaar on the opposite site of the walled city to get a first impression, then explore the lanes leading off left and right, and you will understand that the Ichan-Kala has grown organically and not through urban planning. The span of arches and portals, high walls, light angled towers, cupolas, minarets, and lofty aywans with wooden columns create unexpected silhouettes.

The general view of Khiva
Anton Kovalenko

The ramparts are rare samples of medieval fortification, preserved to the present day. Khiva town was surrounded with two rows of walls, the Ichan-Kala (inner town) and Dishan-Kala (outer town). The wall of Ichan-Kala was created at the turn of the 6th century B.C. and are up to 10m high and 8m thick, built of adobe, capped with toothed railings and pierced by narrow embrasures from which enemy attacks were repulsed. Some of the moats are still visible today, though they are no longer water-filled.

The town gates were also a part of the fortification system. They have the special devices, which were used by the town's protecting guards. On both sides of the arch passage, there are "blowing" towers, above the gate there is an inspection gallery. The passage is covered by an arched roof (Koy-Darvaza), or if the passage is too long, by several cupolas.

On the sides of the passage, there are small rooms, where the sentries and customs officials lived, adjacent to a court room and a prison. Gates and access to public spaces were elaborate in design for a city's prestige was judged by the grandeur of its access. The gates were trimmed with beautiful and multi-coloured glazed tiles and adorned with ayats from the Koran or praise for the Khan. The walls of Ichan-Kala have 4 gates: Ata-Darvaza, Palvan-Darvaza, Tash-Darvaza, and Bagcha-Darvaza.

MINARET ISLAM-HOJA

The minaret was built by the order of Islam-Hoja, the prime minister of the Khan. This minaret is called the symbol of Khiva, its slightly conic shape an early sample of the architecture of ancient Kunya-Urgench from the 14th century. The brickwork is based on a striped pattern from glazed tiles, the height of the minaret is 56.6m with a bottom diameter of 9.5m.

MINARET KALTA MINOR

Planned to become the highest minaret in the Islamic world at 80m, construction of the Kalta Minor was interrupted and the project abandoned, with the death of its commissioner, the Khan himself, in 1855. Thus the proportions between the height of 29m and the bottom diameter of 14.2m are not in line with the magnificent tower the Khiva ruler had in mind. Kalta Minor is, however, the only minaret with the entire surface covered in glazed tiles.

MADRESSA OF SHERGAZI KHAN

Situated in the centre of the Ichan-Kala across from the entrance to the beautiful Pahlavon Mahmud mausoleum, the madressa of Shergazi Khan is listed as the oldest and biggest madressa of Khiva. Its entrance is 2m below street level due to the terrain.

MADRESSA OF MUHAMMAD RAKHIM KHAN II

The full name of the Khan was Said Muhammad Rakhim Bahadur Khan, popularly known as Madrim Khan II. He was the writer and poet under the pseudonym, Feruz. The construction of madressa, which he had built, was completed in 1871 and is one of the largest in the Ichan-Kala. The view onto the madressa from Rakhim Khan's private residence was short lived, for in 1973 Khiva surrendered to the Russians and the Khan fled the city.

MADRESSA OF MUHAMMAD AMIN KHAN

Offering space for over 250 students, the madressa was the biggest in all of Central Asia in the 1850s with hujras on two stories. A first in design, the students' hujras on the second floor each had an annex, allowing for more space while those on the ground floor were open to the outer facade. Beside the theological school, the madressa accommodated the Chancellery of the Muslim Supreme Court.

DJUMA MOSQUE

According to a description by the Arab geographer Al Muqaddasi, the Friady mosque dates from the 10th century. This mosque is unique in its construction; it has no portals, cupolas, galleries or inner yard and access to the mosque is possible from three sides.

The ceiling of the huge hall rests on 213 wooden columns dating from various centuries. Small openings in the ceilings let in light and air. Along the southern wall, niches with stalactites stand out and on the right, curiously

enough, a marble plate indicates profits and estates. The hand carved doors and columns are of special interest for they show different styles and techniques through the ages and some of them are even engraved with the year they were carved, namely 1316, 1517, 1788 and 1789.

UCH AVLIOLI MAUSOLEUM

Situated near the western walls of Tash Hauli, the mausoleum is the resting place of three saints. The huge hall of the mausoleum is covered by a cellular vault cupola, under which rest the remains of the saints. The earliest mazar dates back to 1561 as inscribed on the panel of the entrance door. At the end of the 20th century (1980s) the entrance portal, some of the columns and parts of the aywan were damaged by heavy rains. After restoration and reconstruction the mausoleum has once again become a frequently visited pilgrimage site.

MAUSOLEUM OF SAID ALLAUDDIN

The building of the mausoleum borders upon the eastern walls of the Matniyaz Divan-begi madressa and was built in honour of the famous Sufi sheikh in 1303. The burial vault, with its cupola and its unique majolica headstone, is dated to the first half of the 14th century. A zioratkhona, the place where adepts of Sufism hold their zikr rituals, was added in the 17th century.

KUNYA ARK

The old fortress Kunya Ark connects the western wall of Ichan-Kala with the abode of the hermit, Ak Sheikh Bobo. The construction of Kunya Ark was undertaken around 1686-1688 by Arang Khan, the son of Anush Khan. At the end of the 18th century, Kunya Ark became a "town within a town", and was separated from the Ichan-Kala by a high wall. At one time the fortress consisted of a multi yard complex encompassing the Khan's chancellery, reception hall, harem, winter and summer mosques, and the mint and barns (stable, storehouses, workshops, powder mill). The present day structure of Kunya Ark in its restored state stems from the 19th century. The square near the entrance to Kunya Ark was used for military parades and training battles.

There were also a special place for serving a sentence and a zindan (prison), bordering upon the eastern walls of Kunya Ark. What remains of the former vast estate are the eastern gate with its guard room and the Kurinish khona reception hall and aywan with anti chamber from the 1680s, though this was destroyed by Iranian invaders in the 18th century and subsequently reconstructed and adorned with beautiful majolica under Alla Kuli Khan. It is here that the Khan, seated on his throne, received his subjects, dignitaries and delegations, adjacent to the treasury and the archive for manuscripts. The wood carved throne, along with its silver ornaments, is now on display at the Moscow Museum. In the middle of the courtyard a traditional felt yurt provided the correct venue to receive ambassadors of nomadic tribes.. Some of the best photos of Khiva can shot at sunset from the Akshik Bobo ayvan high above the palace.

TASH HAULI PALACE

The palace is situated in the eastern part of Khiva and was built between 1830 and 1838 by Alla Kuli Khan under the architectural leadership of Usto Kalandar Hivagi. Situated opposite his magnificent, and recently splendidly restored, madressa, it features prime examples of exquisite geometric majolica compositions by a master craftsman, Abdulloh. The main purpose of the Tash Hauli was to provide a living quarter for the ladies of the harem to which was added the mehmonkhona (reception area) and finally an arzikhona (courtroom). On the southern part of the harem's inner courtyard, four small aywans each belonged to one of the four official wives according to sharia law, with the fifth aywan reserved exclusively for the Khan himself. The Harem was constructed according to the Khorezmian tradition of "the women's side" (ichan hauli). The work was done by the famous master Abdullah, nicknamed "The Genius". This master decorated all the yards in Tash Hauli. The period of the Alla Kuli Khans is characterized by strong governmental skills, successful international politics and progress in trade with Russia.

Khiva. Old city
Anton Kovalenko

MAP OF KHIVA

1 Isfandiyar Palace

2 Kheivak Well

3 Zindan

4 Mohammed Rakhim Khan Madressa

5 Arabkhana Madressa

6 Dost Alimjob Madressa

7 Dost Alyam Madressa

8 Tash Khauli Palace

9 Alloquli Khan Caravan Serai

10 Alloquli Khan Madressa

11 Kutlimurodinok Madressa

12 Matpana Bay Madressa

13 Kalta Minor Madressa

14 Sayid Alauddin Mausoleum

15 Qoli Kalon Madressa

16 Juma Mosque

17 Juma Minaret

18 Abdulla Khan Madressa

19 Ak Mosque

20 Anusha Khan Mosque

21 Islam Khodja Madressa

22 Islam Khodja Minaret

23 Pakhlavon Muhammed Mausoleum

24 Shergozi Khan Madressa

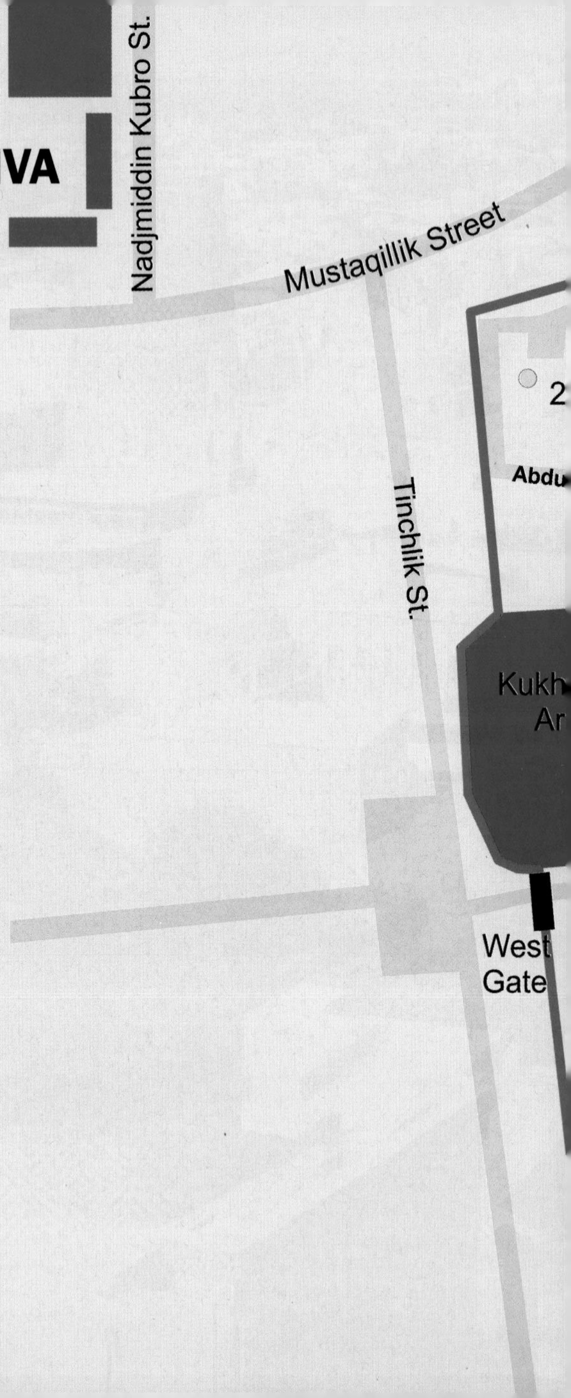

Nadjmiddin Kubro St.

Mustaqillik Street

Tinchlik St.

2

Abdu

Kukh
Ar

West
Gate

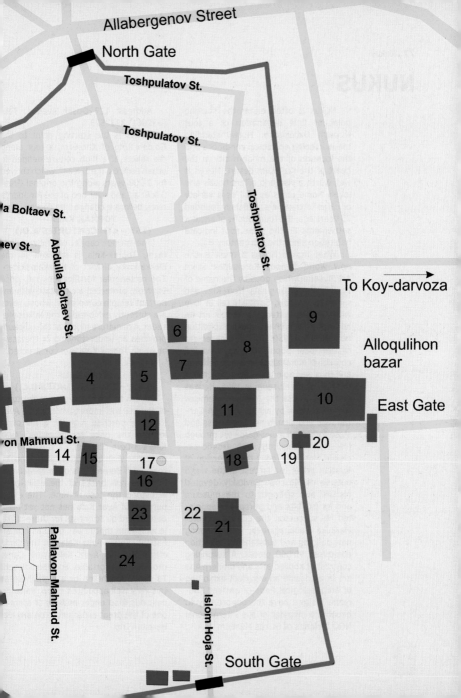

NUKUS

Nukus is often either the starting point or final destination of a tour through Uzbekistan. Notwithstanding the worsening ecological conditions and the location of the modern city in the heart of the Kizil Kum desert, Nukus is well worth a visit and offers hotels and lovely home stays as well as a variety of cafes to travellers. Officially founded 75 years ago, the foundations of ancient settlements on the same spot indicate habitation since the 4th century B.C.

What makes Nukus a must is the now world famous Karakalpak State Art Museum which goes by the name of Igor Savitskiy. Originally from Kiev and raised in Moscow, Savitskiy fell in love with Karakalpakstan and its folk art on an important archaeological expedition he joined in 1950. To the amazement of the local population, he salvaged objects of Karakalpak cultural heritage and thus was able to become director of the new State Museum in 1966. He was also able to use the museum premises to collect work by artists living in Central Asia and simultaneously amass and store forbidden avant-garde art through his close connections with artistic circles in Moscow. Today the collection of Russian art is the largest in the world outside of Moscow. Savitskiy devoted his life and strength to the museum and its exhibits and personally appointed his successor, the current director Marinika Babanazarova. The stunning new building and outstanding collection comprises 90'000 pieces. A surprising contrast of applied arts and modern fine art sit alongside an excellent exhibition of archaeological finds of ancient Khorezm. Visitors have the opportunity to become a member of the international NGO "Friends of Nukus Museum".

Address: 127 Doslik Avenue. Tel. (+99861) 2222573

Nukus is the starting point to the Golden Ring of Khorezm, a tour along the relicts of a high culture defined in urban centres, the "kalas", which thrived for 2'000 years along the original Great Silk Road and river bed of the Amudarya river, before it changed its course.

TOPRAK KALA
(1ST – 4TH CENTURIES A.D.)

The former capital of ancient Khorezm, Toprak-Kala is situated in the Ellikkalinsky district of Karakalpakstan. The rectangular fortification wall, once 9m high, protected a city state with important temple complexes, whose relics are currently exhibited at the Nukus Museum. A miniature model at the museum provides an understanding of the scale at which Toprak Kala was constructed.

AYAZ KALA
(4TH – 2ND CENTURIES B.C.)

40 km to the north-east of the town of Beruni, the impressive ruins of Ayaz Kala are perched high on a hill overlooking the once fertile plains. Ayaz Kala's 3-tiers cling onto a cliff, and are distinctly visible when approaching by road from Beruni. It is quite miraculous how the raw bricks of the walls have withstood the test of time. The exact purpose of Ayaz Kala has not yet been determined by scientists for there is little indication that it was used as human habitat. Below Ayaz Kala, on the same elevation, the Ayaz Kala Yurt Camp provides comfortable accommodation. To spend lunchtime or a night here at this very well appointed camp, enjoying delicious food under millions of stars is one of the great experiences on any Uzbekistan trip.

Savitsky Museum. New building

BIG GULDURSUN
(5TH – 3RD CENTURIES B.C.)

A mere 20 km to east of Beruni, this huge and well preserved fortress with side walls over 300m long has yielded many objects of daily use such as ceramics, bronze coins, pottery and jewellery.

MIZDAKHKAN (GYAUR-KALA IN KHODJELI) (4TH CENTURY B.C.)

The Ancient Mizdahkan archaeological complex is located on three hills in the south-western suburbs of Khodjeli town. It includes the Gyaur-Kala fortress, the Shamun Nabi mausoleum, the Mazlumkhan Sulu, Khalfa Erejep and a caravanserai. During the archaeological excavations, unique ossuaries (the burial receptacles of Zoroastrians) were unearthed next to coins, household items, glassware and highly artistic objects made from gold. Mizdakhan definitely rates among the most magic and interesting complexes of Khorezm.

The legend about the Mazlumkhan Mausoleum claims that a beautiful girl by the name of Mazlumkhan and a builder fell in love with each other. To prove his love, the builder set out to erect the highest tower in her honour. When Mazlumkhan's father, however, refused to allow his daughter to marry the ambitious builder, the desperate couple jumped together from that very tower to meet a sad ending. Another legend recounts the story of the Caliph Erejep claiming the mausoleum to be the tomb of a holy man who strongly propagated the religion of Islam

at its earliest stage. The remaining walls testify to its former impressive size. According to yet another legend, Adam's grave is to be found at the same spot. Near the entrance of the mausoleum is a pile of baked bricks. It is said that each year one baked brick falls down from the wall and the day the last brick drops is to be doomsday. No need to worry just yet though, the walls of the mausoleum are rather high and thus doomsday will not arrive any time soon!

CHILPIK
(2ND – 4TH CENTURIES A.D.)

Off the road from Khiva to Nukus, 43km before Nukus, a circular silhouette is perceived against the southern horizon. The conic hill is 40m high and represents the remains of a former Zoroastrian temple and burial site, which can still be climbed today.

JAMPYK KALA
(4TH – 6TH CENTURIES A.D.)

6 km to the south-east of Karatau village, off the road and behind the first chain of south-western Sultanuizdag's black mountain range, this fantastic, pink coloured citadel is well worth the detour. Plenty of shards are still to be found and archaeologists have unearthed precious objects from places as far away as China, Egypt, Russia, Europe, and India, an indicator that Jampyk was an important trading point. Indeed, Jampyk is adjacent to a branch of the Amudarya river in what is today the Baday Tugay nature reserve. The settlement used to serve as a port with barges transporting goods in large quantities both north and south.

The Rain. 1920. Irina Shtange. Museum Savitsky

NATURE OF UZBEKISTAN

The exotic nature of Uzbekistan with its surprising contrasts, variety of flora and fauna and favourable climate (there are plenty of sunny days in the year) attracts numerous numbers of ecological tourists. There are ten natural reserves in Uzbekistan, which accommodate a variety of unique landscapes from velvet sand to flowering oases, including stunning scenery from the Tugai River to Alpine plains, the desert lake Aydarkul, the lofty glacier Fedchenko or the surviving coniferous woods on the Pskem mountainside.

BADAI-TUGAI NATURE RESERVE

The Badai-Tugai reserve was established in the Karakalpak Autonomous Republic in 1971. It covers an area of 6,497 hectares and is situated in the lower reaches of the Amudarya, on the territories of Beruniy and Kegeyliy, on the right bank of the river.

Plenty of water and a variety of nesting places attracts an amazing array of birds. Migrant birds such as the spotted flycatcher, common redstart, black redstart, common redbreast, tawny pipit, rose-colored starling, rock sparrow, brisk, siskin and others inhabit the territory of the reserve. During winter time it is home to the goshawk, the East-Siberian hawk, marsh owl, black lark, for different species of thrush, and grosbeak. Among settled birds one can see the common kestrel, rock pigeons, laughing doves, horned owls, long-eared owls, crested larks, Bukhara great tit, common mylady's-belt, and tree sparrows. The most important bird of the reserve is the Khiva pheasant. The Kokdarya channels are inhabited by blue halcyons while the Tugai plains are inhabited by white-winged woodpeckers. The fauna prevailing here includes wild boar, jackals, tolai hares, badgers, foxes, reed cats and hedgehogs. Reservoirs are inhabited by lake frogs, water-snakes while in the grass roam shaft serpents and Pallas' colubers. Spotty and cross-barred racers are found near the ruins of the ancient fortress, Jampir Kala, a considerable place of interest of the reserve.

The fauna of the Amudarya and Kokdarya rivers include about 15 species of fish. The most important of them are shovel-nosed Aral barbel, bream, sazan, cat-fish, grass carp and silver carp.

In 1975 Bukhara Deer, two does and a buck, were released into the reserve for the purpose of breeding this almost extinct species. Now they number around 260.

The Hissar reserve was established in 1994 and its current territory occupies 80,986 hectares. It is situated in a typical mountainous area with lots of canyons and karst caves, mountain streams, water-falls and small glaciers. Predominant in the forest belt is the Zerafshan conifer and in the higher territories the hemispherical conifer. Flora species of these coniferous woods include mostly broad-leaved trees such as the Turkestani maple, barberry and brier as well as Semyonov maple, Bukhara almond-tree, common and Regel pear, the Persian Rowan-tree and others. At a height of 2,400m you can see coniferous elfin wood, high-mountain bunchgrass steppe and meadows. Overall, the flora of the reserve includes 490 species of plants.

Common mammals that inhabit this territory are long-tailed marmot, tolai hare, porcupine, wolf, fox, white-clawed bear, snow leopard and others. It is also home for birds such as bearded vulture, Himalayan and black

A gecko
Alexander Yesipov

griffons, golden eagle, eagle-owl and many others. In the South of the reserve, in the valley of the Kalasay River, the well known cave named after Amir Temur (Tamerlane Cave) with an underground lake, stalactites and stalagmites, as well as a rock with dinosaurs' footprints are fascinating sites to visit. In the North lie several small glaciers such as Severtsov and Batirbay.

ZAMIN MOUNTAIN-CONIFEROUS NATURE RESERVE

Established in 1960 in order to protect the unique coniferous forests inhabited by endemic flora and fauna, the reserve covers an area of 10.5 hectares, of which 4,161 hectares are forests. The nature reserve is situated in the Jizzak region of Uzbekistan, between Tashkent and Samarkand. The flora includes several hundred species, many of which are used for household purposes and present an important gene pool. They contain: medicinal herbs, balsamiferous, tanniferous, tinctorial, ethereal, fruit and pabular plants.

The mountain-steppe belt of the reserve is inhabited by Turkestani agama, Pallas' coluber, desert lidless skink, glass-snake, coniferous tit, Himalayan tree creeper, blue-capped redstart, wolf, tolai hare and common mole-vole.

The forest belt is home to the green toad, lake frog and mamushi whereas the coniferous area is mostly rich in birds. The common birds you see here are: yellow-hammers, chanters, thrush, redstart, coniferous grosbeak, turtle-dove, ring-dove, Turkestani eagle-owl, and Turkestani starling. The canyons of the waterfalls are inhabited by bluebirds and blue tits while the stony banks are inhabited by common and brown dippers, common sandpiper and wagtail and lastly the rocks are inhabited by prey birds such as griffon vulture, black vulture and lammergeyers.

In the heart of the forest you can meet white-claw bear, Turkestani lynx, forest dormouse, Karuters field-vole, forest mouse and dwarf hamster; while on the uncovered cliffs and slide-rocks you meet stone-martens.

ZERAFSHAN VALLEY-TUGAI NATURE RESERVE

The Zerafshan nature reserve was created in 1975 in the Samarkand region. Occupying 2,352 hectares it is located in the flood lands of the Zerafshan River in the Bulungur and Jambay regions of Samarkand, typical of a valley and flood-tugai reserve. Asiatic poplar, oleaster, sea-buckthorn, tamarisk, willow, woodreed, reed mace, reed-oleaster, motley grass and rush are assimilated here, as are apple-trees, common pears, common apricot-tree, peach, walnuts and vine. It is the only place where sea-buckthorn grows openly on the plains. For over 1000 years, these floodlands have been inhabited by pheasants. Add to this halcyon, white-winged woodpecker, laughing dove, carrion-crow, rook, magpie, Bukhara tit, common starling, my-lady's-belt, crested lark, tree sparrow; hobby falcon, golden bee-eaters, scops-owl, and scrub robins throughout the summer months and during winter white and common heron, buzzard, sparrow-hawk, grosbeak, hooded crow, wren, black-throated thrush and blackbird.

At night, the badger, pea shrub, jackal, jungle cat, porcupine and marbled polecat are active.

Since 1995 the nature reserve has enjoyed the support of the National Centre on Ecological Researches (CNRS), the Embassy of France in Uzbekistan, the International Association for the promotion of cooperation with scientists from the independent states of the former Soviet Union (INTAS), J. and K. Macarthur's Funds, World Wildlife Fund (WWF) and Holland Government, and European Initiatives on Large Herbivorous (LHI) for the reproduction of Bukhara deer. Since 1999, deer reproduction in its entirety has been supported by a project sponsored by WWF. In 2005 the first group of Bukhara deer was given their freedom from the open-air cages, where they had been raised.

KITAB GEOLOGICAL PRESERVE

Kitab Geological Preserve, covering 5,378 hectares of the Kitab region of Kashkadarya, was established in 1979. The government took under its protection the mountainous landscape that captures life spanning over 400 million years.

The administrative building of the reserve exhibits paleontological finds and more recent species of flora and fauna.

By 1978, within the entire geo-chronological area of the reserve, geologists had gathered information about 700 fossilized species of such widespread groups such as stromatoporoideas, tabulate and helio-lithoidals, rugosis, brachiopods, moss animalcules, trilobites, seed shrimps, cystoideas and crinotropics, pelitipods, algae, blastoideas, goniatites, graptolites, fish and 500 species of plants. The fauna has 21 species of mammals and 120 species of birds, of which the golden eagle, bearded vulture, booted eagle and others are included in the Red Book of Uzbekistan.

KIZILKUM TUGAI-SAND NATURE RESERVE

The reserve was established in 1971 and is located along the riverside of the Amudarya. It covers an area of 10,311 hectares, of which 5,144 are forests, 6,964 are sandy areas and 3,177 hectares are flood-land of the river. The forest part of the reserve is a natural plantation of trees. The flora counts 103 species of plants, including white saxaul, Euphratean poplar, willows, oleaster, tamarisk, adder's-spear, cirsomphalos and desert herbs.

On takyr soil you can meet bur, black saxaul and wormwood. Ethemers are rare to this area. The alluvial-bog soil is full of reeds.

The fauna is far more diverse and typical of that found in riverside valleys and sandy-desert areas. It includes 197 species of birds, 37 species of mammals and 23 species of reptiles. The reserve is also home to the Bukhara deer although they are rarely seen in the sandy areas of the reserve, which are commonly inhabited by tolai hares, wild boars, foxes and wolves. Plenty of birds are common to this area such as marbled duck, golden eagle and black kite and most notably the fascinating Amudarya pheasant. The reserve is also home to steppe turtles, racers, boas and eared hedgehog, as well as poisonous snakes such as the lebetina viper. In the Amudarya river, sazan, barbell, cat-fish and rudd are found aplenty.

A hedgehog
Anton Kovalenko

NURATA NATURE RESERVE

Situated in the Jizzak region (Farish, Khayas village), in the northern mountainside of Nuratau, the Nurata nature reserve was established to protect the population of rare species of fauna such as the Severtsov sheep and important types of walnuts.

The area of the reserve occupies 17,752 hectares, of which 2,529 hectares are forests. The nature reserve is crossed by ten not intermittent big and small streams.

The flora of the reserve is unique and counts 600 species of plants. The fauna is diverse and includes Pallas' coluber, mountain and red-banded racers, lebetina viper, copperhead snake, steppe turtles and steppe agama, glass-snake, Turkestani gecko, turkestani agama, long-legged skink and barred wolf snake. One migration route of birds crosses through the Nuratau Mountains. The reserve is constantly inhabited by birds such as Indian starling, kekliks, golden eagles, white-headed griffons, black vulture, black chats and gray-necked buntings.

There are also a large number of mammals here. The common ones include pea shrub, desert wolf, corsac fox, stone marten, porcupine, tolai-hare, boar, forest dormouse, long-legged hedgehog, red-tailed and great gerbil, Severtsov's jerboa and Severtsov's sheep.

SURKHAN FOREST-MOUNTAIN NATURE RESERVE

It covers an area of 24,554 hectares, of which 9,284 are forests and is located in the South-West branches of the Hissar Mountains as part of the Pamir-Alay mountainous system.

The flora here includes over 800 species of plants, of which tricuspid spurge, wild vine, Bukhara bean caper and others are unique to this area. There are 290 species of birds including Turkestani white and black storks, bearded vulture, golden eagle, Barbary falcon, serpent eagle, white-headed griffon, black vulture and others; 37 species of mammals of which markhor, Bukhara argali, striped hyena, Bukhara deer and Turkestani lynx are under special protection. The rare reptiles of the area include gray lizard, Central-Asian cobra, barred wolf snake and Afghan winkles.

In the conservation zone of the reserve you can see cultural and historical monuments. In the southern part of Baysuntau there is a well-known grotto, Teshik-Tash, where the skeleton of a Neanderthal boy was found.

CHATKAL FOREST-MOUNTAIN BIOSPHERE RESERVE

The reserve was established in 1947 and occupies 35.2 hectares. The territory of the reserve consists of two areas, Bashkizilsay and Maydantal - separated from each other by mountain passes. Maydantal is hardly accessible and can be reached only by walking or horseback.

The flora of the reserve includes over 40 species of woody and shrubby plants. Part of them is endemic to the Western Tien-Shan. Most of the reserve is covered by natural coniferous forests. There are two species of coniferous plants here: on the river banks birchwoods and among shrubby plants black currant, Turkestani mountain ash, Magaleb cherry-tree, pistachio-tree and others. Among trees you will find Afghan poplar, willows, Semyonov maple, Caucasian hackberry, walnut, Severtsov apple-tree, cherry-plum, alycha and apricot-tree. The fauna consists of Siberian ibex, boars, roe deer, turkestani lynx, white-claw bears, foxes, stone martens, marmots, porcupines, ermines, Tien Shan sousliks and snow leopards.

The reserve is inhabited by the following birds: keklik, snowcock, partridge, black vulture, white-headed griffon, bearded vulture, and golden eagle. In the mountain rivers you can meet marinka, Amudarya loach, and Turkestani small catfish.

ADVENTURE TOURISM IN UZBEKISTAN

The world-renowned monuments of Samarkand, Bukhara, Khiva and other ancient cities attract each year hundreds of tourists to Uzbekistan from all over the world. However, until present the richest natural potential of Uzbekistan has been hardly touched.

On the territory of Uzbekistan, some of the greatest deserts of Asia can be found, namely the Kizilkum (The Red Sand), the mysterious Ustyurt plateau, the mountains of the Pamir-Alay and Tien Shan reaching heights of more than 4500m above sea level.

The natural riches of Uzbekistan, in combination with a favourable climate, make for excellent itineraries for many kinds of excursions not only through ecological tourism but also for adventurous holidays: trekking, cycling and equestrian tourism, skiing and snow boarding, heli-skiing, rafting, camel safaris and off road tours. The most famous place for an adventurous holiday is the Chimgan mountains. Being only 80km away from Uzbekistan's capital, the area geographically belongs to the south-western Tien Shan mountain range. The Big Chimgan, with its dominant height (3309m), "takes off" its snow cap only at the end of the summer, so skiers can ski up to the end of June!

In the winter, Chimgan is a true Alpine skiing resort. Certainly, as for the quantity and quality of the mountain ski routes, Chimgan and the neighbouring Alpine skiing resort "Beldersay" are inferior to those in Europe but experts have appreciated the most slippery snow in the world, as well as great possibilities for free riding, and especially for heli-skiing. Many fans of extreme mountain skiing consider the Chimgan mountains among the best all over the world for this purpose and every year come here to travel by helicopter to inaccessible heights and compete with speed in the wind, descending through untouched soft snow. There are not many places in the world where your own private slope is up to 2km wide, at a length of up to 10km, covering in one day "16 vertical kilometres" (almost twice the height of the Everest).

During summer time, Chimgan is a vast expanse for Alpinists and trekking fans. Picturesque canyons, waterfalls, the mysterious Polatkhan plateau, the ravines of the river Karaarcha, boundless mountain ranges, and rock paintings, all these remain in tourists' memory for a lifetime.

Chimgan also offers horse routes through the same mountains.

Here, along the Chatkal, Pskem, and Ugam rivers, you can try white water rafting and challenge yourself to conqueror the perilous "white water". If Chatkal and Pskem are the rivers for the professionals, then Ugam is subdued enough so that even the average white water fan can have great fun and experience an adrenalin rush.

Another interesting place for the adventurous holiday is the Nuratinsk mountain range. Though not very high at 1500 – 2500m above sea level, in the spring it is a wonderful place for trekking, riding, and biking. Besides, this place is interesting also from the point of view of ethnography and for rural tourism.

A wide territory that seems devoid of life at first but actually offers plenty of recreational activities is the Kizilkum desert, with its camel safari, jeep and off-road tours. It is striking to hear that there are many lakes in the desert, and the biggest among them is lake Aydarkul (more than 200km in length and up to 15km in width). Thousands of birds and excellent fishing make this an ideal recreation area. The yurt camp «Aydar» on the western shores enjoys increasing popularity, year by year, for it is the starting point of camel rides and visits of one of the biggest stone picture "galleries" of the early man with over 3,000 petroglyphs.

Travelling up to the region of the disappearing Aral Sea is an adventure trip more in the style of an adventurous expedition and requires in depth preparation, desert proof transportation and knowledgeable local guides. Those who have indeed approached the Aral Sea from its western shores speak of a touching and unforgettable trip to an area that is slowly where desertification is the key factor to the change in landscape.

Only few are aware of the possibilities within Uzbekistan for sports fishing. Fast mountain rivers, man-made canals, the greatest Asian rivers Syrdaria and Amudarya, and lakes in the deserts are the venues that can be offered to fishing enthusiasts. Along with the traditional fish species from all over the world, such as sazan, barbel, carp, pike, perch, cat-fish and bream, there is the chance to fish for species that are typically only found in Central Asia, such as dragon head, marinka, tupak, and Samarkand khromulya. Fishing in all reservoirs is also for sport using a fishing rod, and spinning either from the shore or a boat.

Adventurous holidays in the mountains, including hiking and meeting local inhabitants are the very elements that exhilarate and add to the traditional culture tours through Uzbekistan. Many tour operators now include these unforgettable adventures in the list of their services.

UZBEKISTAN'S NATIONAL CUISINE

"In the East. In the East, what is life without a haikhana?...". Many locals hum the words of this song and it is true. Uzbek people do not only like to eat but also to prepare delicious food. For the dear guest, the host rolls up his sleeves and cooks the main national dish, "plov", serving this local rice dish on the dastarhan (table-cloth) in a large, hand painted lyagan plate.

All regions have their own traditional plov, these is Tashkent, Jizzak, Samarkand, Bukhara, and hiva plov. Each of these areas has their very own distinct recipe to prepare the delicious dish. Plov is always accompanied by salads from fresh vegetables, syuzma and chakka (dairy specialties made from buttermilk) as the perfect counter balance to the richness of the dish.

Plov can be cooked with heads of garlic, raihns, almonds, peas and quince. Adding various ingredients depends on the imagination of the cook, who is, among people, respectively named "osh-paz".

The plov course is always followed by hot and aromatic green tea.

At many B&B's and hotels the hosts prepare the plov in the kazan, an almost hemispherical pot before you and with your direct participation. But during sight-seeing you will become the witness of its preparation in the streets near the restaurants, cafes and chaikhana tea houses. In Tashkent alone, at lunch time, there are several plov centres operating and always drawing a large crowd of faithful customers.

The main peculiarity of plov is probably the fact that its cooks are mostly men. While cooking, Uzbek men are very lavish, they put more ingredients than are really needed, especially more meat, the major feature of Uzbek cuisine.

However, if you visit grocery stores in Tashkent, it may seem that the traditional food of Uzbek people is ravioli. Now don't get confused. The mantys are the analogy of raviolis in Uzbekistan. They are steamed dumplings cooked in a special pot and bigger than raviolis. Stuffing for manty is diced potato or cut meat with onion and spices. Meat prepared for the filling of the mantys is never minced, it is cut into tiny pieces so that the meat stays juicy and does not lose its aroma and flavour.

There is no way to imagine how tasty soups are in Uzbekistan. The rich shurpa with mutton or beef for instance. Shurpa is served in a kosa (deep bowl) that is full of golden broth with bite size pieces of meat, small cloves of potato and carrots. In spite of arguments about the origin of macaroni, it is most likely that it was invented in the East. The interlacing of traditions and cultures on the Great Silk Road can be observed even in cookery. Taste lagman, the ancestor of modern spaghetti in its original environment. The preparation technology of this long vermicelli is very difficult and mastered only by skilled chefs. The vermicelli are bounced back and forth through the air with very specific flicks of the wrist and are entirely handmade. Many cafes offer Uzbek and Uyghur lagman.

There are some soups that are typical only to Uzbek cuisine. They are kurtova, shopirma, kakurum, sihmon. Their preparation is based on dairy products and they originated from the nomadic ancestors of Uzbek people.

You will be amazed to see plenty of snack-bars serving pastries in Tashkent. Most of them prepare and sell not only traditional pastries but also samsa. Genuine samsa is baked in a tandyr clay oven, with the baking process being an art form in itself. To throw the filled dough triangle onto the interior clay wall of the hot tandyr where it sticks until it is ready and to know when to remove the baked triangle from that clay wall before it falls off on its own into the flames, requires talent and skill. In the hills outside of Jizzak, along the road from Tashkent to Samarkand, at Bahmal village, the way side chaikhanas are famous for a delicacy you should try without fail: tandyr-kebab, mutton braised in the wood burning clay oven, whose aroma is enhanced with juniper tree branches.

Fried fish is popular in many places of Uzbekistan, especially in the "coastal" regions along the lakes and rivers.

And last but not least, let us mention shashlyk, which is served in almost all cafes and restaurants. There are different kinds of shashlyk, from mutton, beef, chicken, fish and liver, both in morsels and as ground meat. Note that the more fat on the meat the better the shashlyk is considered as the flavour is enhanced.

Finally, sweets, beverages and fruits are the customary attribute of the Uzbek dastarkhan, the fully laid out table for guests. In Europe, sweets are served for dessert after the main course, but in the East sweets are eaten twice, sometimes even three times - before, during and after the main course.

Tea is just as important as fruits, grapes, berries and melon during dinner in Uzbekistan. Dinner begins with having a bowl of tea; tea is served with rich dishes and tea finishes a dinner and is drunk with sweets. People from different regions prefer different kinds of tea. In most parts of Uzbekistan in the East and South (Bukhara, Samarkand, Fergana Valley) people drink green tea, while in Tashkent and the Northern regions of Uzbekistan black tea is preferred. Other typical beverages prepared for the Uzbek dastarkhan are sherbets fruit syrup with sugar.

In case anyone thought the Russian hangover had passed, many Uzbeks, despite their Muslim heritage, are heavy alcoholic drinkers enjoying vodka drunk with numerous toasts. There is quite a lot of pressure to down each shot poured, so be prepared for a heavy night with locals. Russian and European beers are also available, and occasionally you find a good local beer, which, if it is served cold, is welcome relief from the summer heat.

In general Uzbek sweets can be divided into six groups: kiyoms (fruity and vegetable syrups), bekmeses (concentrated fruit and berry juices and molasses), navvats (different types of crystallized boiled grape sugar with dyes and spices), and sweets based on raisins and nuts, and at last different halvahs and halvah-like sweet stuff.

Cooking samsa
Anton Kovalenko

Plov
Central Asia travel

CULTURE AND TRADITIONS OF UZBEKISTAN

The Uzbek nation is one of the most ancient and vital nations in the world.

In the 4th century B.C. the inhabitants of the lands of Uzbekistan changed their nomadic lifestyle and settled in these fertile areas. At the dawn of civilization, settlers thus made a distinctive culture their own which has remained to some extent largely similar to that of the times of Darius and Alexander the Great. Even the migration of entire peoples through its territory or the intrusion of the Mongolians did not dilute that local culture. Only Islam, introduced with the Arab conquest, had a slight influence on the Uzbek people, yet it did not override the essence of Uzbek culture but rather blended in to harmonize with existing values.

Naturally, modern life and globalization brought changes, but most Uzbek families still honour the ways of their forefathers. The common Uzbek family consists of several generations of relatives living together. There is a specific hierarchy, all members obey the head of the family and respect the elderly. An Uzbek woman, on the one hand, is wife and mother, but on the other hand, the subordinate of the husband's father and mother. But it is not perceived as discrimination, it is an ancient tradition based on life. Children are the most loved members of the family.

"Mahalla" is a community of neighbours living in one street, part of town or village, with their own institutions of local governing and its own subculture and traditions - the traditional form of social order.

The noblest tradition is "khashar", mutual aid. The customary tradition is that of hospitality. Adhering to the code of welcoming one's guests is more valuable than the wealth of the host. Do not refuse your host's invitation for dinner or you may hurt his feelings. While visiting a home it is customary to present souvenirs or sweets for the children. The host will likely meet you at the gate, greet you, ask about your business and life and invite you inside. Guests are welcomed in the reception room or in the yard. When you enter the living quarters take off your shoes. The richly laid-out table "dastarkhan" is placed at the centre of the room, veranda or in the yard under the trees or vines.

The seats farthest from the gate or entrance are the most honourable ones. Usually women sit separately from men, but in cities this rule is rarely kept. Dinner commences and finishes by drinking tea. Sweets, pastry, dried fruits, nuts, fresh fruits and vegetables are served as appetizers and at the end of dinner. Also, plov or another main dish is served for guests. It is obligatory that round flat bread (lepyoshka) is broken and placed on the dastarkhan.

The essential part of every dinner is the tea-drinking ceremony. Preparing and serving tea is the prerogative of men, entirely of the host. Tea is infused in the tea-pot and

National dance
Photo: Koval

poured into pyalas (small bowls). A humble amount of tea in a pyala is the sign of utmost hospitality so the more honourable the guest is, the less tea is in his pyala. For a guest to hold out the empty pyala for extra tea means he is paying tribute to the host. Accordingly, uninvited guests are served a full pyala of tea, so you will know when it is time to leave!

Islam plays the most significant part of life in Uzbek families. The religion exists in both private and family life; it also influences the art and the way of people's life in public.

But some traditions are different from traditional Islamic rules. For instance, the obligatory visit to Mecca in Saudi Arabia can be replaced by a pilgrimage to the "sacred places". There are some customs such as "beshik-tuyi", khatna-kilish (customs regarding the birth and upbringing of the child), "fatiha-tuy" engagement (traditions regarding marriage), "sunnat tuy" (customs regarding weddings), "sabzi-tugrar" (traditions regarding preparation of the meal), which are unique to the region. These traditions often show the intertwining of Islamic canons with pre-Islamic practice.

Notwithstanding the strong Islamic traditions, many Uzbek people drink alcoholic beverages, especially with guests as a form of hospitality. If you do not drink strong beverages, mostly vodka and cognac, just let the host know before the meal and although your glass will be filled you will not be expected to consume your drink after the obligatory toast.

Uzbek people are very accessible. It is customary to shake hands while greeting (except woman, unless she first extends her hand). While shaking hands you will be asked about your health, business and life. There is also another way of greeting, namely putting the right hand on the heart and bowing the head.

Uzbek national clothes in many parts of the country have not really changed. Men wear straight-cut shirts and padded coats "chapan" held closed by a handkerchief tied around the waist.

Uzbek men commonly wear dark coloured chapans but occasionally you will see striped ones or for special occasions, the luxurious golden-embroidered chapans. Women wear the voluminous national dress, often made from "khan-atlas" and straight-cut wide trousers. Men's head-dresses are "kalpok", "dopi" "duppi", "sanama", "chizma", "takh'ya", "taykha", "chumakli", "kush" or "kulokhi" (types of skull-caps), women wear colourful scarves. The kids' skull-caps "kulokhcha", "kalpakcha", "duppi", "kalapush" are by far more diverse, embroidered and colorful with splendid brushes, pon-pons and amulets. The skull-caps of different regions vary from each other in their forms, design and colour.

Taking into account the influence of the world's fashions, most people in big cities and villages keep abreast of the times, especially young people. Nevertheless famous Uzbek embroideries and embroidered clothes, traditional head-dresses and carpets are still in great esteem and much preferred over the European style.

CULTURE OF UZBEKISTAN

The culture of Uzbekistan is among the most outstanding and distinctive in the East. It is dominated by folk music, dance and painting.

Uzbek national musical art is distinctive by its variety of subjects and genres. Songs and instrumental tunes can be divided into two parts: songs that are performed during a pre-defined time frame and for a specific ritual context and songs for any occasion.

The first group includes songs concerning customs, working processes, different ceremonies, theatrical performances and games. The Uzbek nation is famous for its many songs. "Koshuk" is the common song consisting of couplets and requiring a small diapason of a melody, which encompasses one or two strophes of the poetic text. "Lapar" and "yalla" have common features with koshuk. They are also couplet songs. This genre requires singing a song while performing a dance with the aim of producing a comical effect. Lapar is a dialogue set to a tune. In Khorezm a song performed by one singer is considered a lapar. In some regions the terminology lapar is used regarding songs performed during wedding celebrations.

Yalla includes two kinds of songs: a small diapason of the melody and introduction to a solo synchronized with dancing. The heritage of famous Eastern poetry is the underlying text accentuated by a melody. Essentially, the most advanced forms of "ashula" are the genre of oral traditional music performed by a professional ensemble. "Dastans", epic legends of lyric heroic content - hold a distinctive place in the Uzbek musical heritage. "Makoms" are intonated classic Persian poetry mixed with the Jewish heritage of Bukhara and "Shashmakom" is a cycle of six makoms, throughout which the players and singers fall into a trance and which performed in its entirety will take up the greater part of a day.

UZBEK ARTS AND CRAFTS

The arts and crafts of Uzbekistan have enjoyed well-earned fame for centuries. The pre-eminence of applied arts can be attributed to historical conditions, such as the emergence of urban oasis and a bourgeoisie who had the means to beautify their homes, shaping the cultural development of the Uzbek people. Uzbeks have developed their technical and artistic traditions over centuries. The applied art reflects everyday life; its main attribute is the close connection between artistic creativity and daily material necessity.

The social nature of decorative art lies in its collectivity. Art is the heritage of many generations; it represents a series of consecutive layers, which reflect people's culture through the ages. The skills and knowledge imparted by various ethnic groups that eventually came together to constitute the Uzbek nation created this diversity of artistic traditions that is the distinguishing feature in works of art of all genres.

GANCH

This architectural-decorative art holds a prominent place in the arts and crafts of Uzbekistan. Principles of ornamental construction and profound knowledge of the plastic and artistic properties of local building materials that were well-known throughout the Middle East, such as ganch (a sort of alabaster), wood, stone, and ceramics, constitute the time-tested fundamentals of this ancient art. The world famous architectural monuments of Bukhara, Samarkand, Khiva, and other cities of Uzbekistan testify to the professional mastery of mediaeval artists and architects, ornamental designers and calligraphers, engravers and ceramists.

WALL PAINTINGS

In Uzbekistan, wall painting and sculptural carving as well as ornamental carving and painting have been practiced since the early medieval periods. The 9th and 10th centuries saw a period of particularly intensive development of ornamental, floral-vegetal polychromatic paintings and relief carving. The more elaborate use of ornamental forms and compositions formed the basis for principles approved by experts through the ages and are observed and adhered to even nowadays.

"Nakkshi" masters of ornamental painting usually practiced ganch and wood architectural painting simultaneously. The most noted masters of wall painting were the Bukhara nakkshi of the last century. Certain private Bed & Breakfasts in Bukhara display the art of nakkshi in their guest rooms.

LACQUERED MINIATURE PAINTING

The production of papier mâché and lacquer painting on papier mâché thrived in Samarkand at the beginning of the 15th century, after the introduction of the art of paper making, testified by sets of genuine ornamental papier mâché medallions found miraculously preserved inside of the Gur Emir mausoleum and the Bibi Khanum mosque. Of special interest is the completely restored golden-blue dome in the interior of the main hall of Gur Emir, composed of 998 papier mâché elements, of which 112 are original and have since been the object of painstaking restoration. There are reasonable grounds for conjecture that it was Samarkand artists who introduced this skill to North India in the 15th century, where it has developed and is nowadays flourishing. Papier mâché articles: pencil-boxes of various sizes, expensive book-covers, chess, caskets, boxes of different sorts, vases, and other small items, were decorated with miniature vegetative patterns. Inscriptions were often incorporated into the ornamentation on pencil-boxes. The paint was applied with thin brushes on a base made of gold or bronze powder, sheet gold and bronze on an apricot and cherry glue. The preparation of lacquers and colours for papier mâché was and still is a sophisticated and highly skilled process.

CERAMICS

From the numerous genres of applied arts in Uzbekistan, the decorative ceramic stands out. The first samples found in the Republic by archaeologists date back to antiquity. Throughout the ages the unique expressiveness and restrained elegance of the best of Uzbek ceramics have revealed the genuine creative genius of the nation.

A case with fragment of miniature

There are dishes, lyagans, spherical cups, pialas, kyosas, vases, jugs, pots, and large and small khums, convenient for use and, at the same time, refined in form. Pottery and ceramics have held an eminent role in the culture of the region and still are coveted items for visitors to bring back home. The works are distinguished by skilled workmanship, beauty of form, enchanting ornaments, richly imaginative designs, and a deep sense of the harmony of colour. There are two kinds of decorative ceramics in Uzbekistan: baked terracotta and slip glaze ceramics. The last 100-150 years has seen ceramic centres with their distinct style establishing themselves in Uzbekistan: Ghizhduvan, Shakhrisabz, Samarkand, Tashkent, Rishtan, and Khorezm. Over the last few decades, the works of ceramists from Gurumsarai, Denau, and Chimbai in Kara-Kalpakstan have also gained in popularity.

The ceramics produced in these centres may be differentiated by their two colour groups: blue-white-green and green-brown-yellow. This is mostly due to technical reasons. In the Fergana valley and Khorezm, where the alkaline glaze ishkor is used, blue, white, and green paintings are predominant, because yellow and red colours decompose under the ishkor glaze, whereas the blue and green colours give a set of fine bright and gentle tints. In the areas where lead glaze is used as in Samarkand, Bukhara, and Tashkent, all shades of the yellow-red-brown spectrum are very popular. The ceramic paintings in these districts are defined by their deep, glowing colour range, and at the same time their surprisingly delicate beauty.

KNIVES & SCISSOR MAKING

A less prominent though important branch of metal-working in Uzbekistan is the art of knife-making. The knives are highly sharpened and kept in leather sheaths decorated with metallic plates, embroidery, appliqué, or painting.

Such knives are called "ghuldor pichok", meaning 'elegant, decorated knife'. The forms are various. The blades differ according to where they are made: narrow or wide, straight or curved, as do the shafts: single-piece or composite, wooden or bone, encrusted or painted.

Of the ancient centres of artistic knife-making remain Chust in the Fergana valley, Khiva and the well known black smiths in Bukhara. The latter city is also famous for its handmade scissors in the form of birds.

FABRICS

Fabric design in Uzbekistan is an outstanding example of folk art. The past and present are wonderfully combined - the traditions of ancient folk art interwoven with the knowledge and understanding of modern times. The art of decorative fabric acts as a kind of history book, reflecting its centuries-old development, and embodying the creative work of many thousands of talented masters and weavers. In the second half of the 19th century, in many cities and settlements (Margilan, Namangan, Bukhara, Andizhan, Samarkand, Kitab, Gizhduvan, Urgut, and Besharyk), miscellaneous plain and patterned hand-made cotton, silk, half-silk fabrics of simple and complex texture were designed and produced. This is what we refer to as ikat nowadays. These textiles were turned into items of clothing and interior decoration. Thick cotton and silk, nap velvet – "bakhmal", moiré rep – "adras", "bekasab", and "banoras", the finest and lightest silk shawls "kalgai", rustling and scintillating "shokhs-kanauses"; specific to the area are the satinated "yakruya" and khan-atlases of contrasting colours; Fergana and Samarkand coverlets with their misty patterns were particularly famous. The ornamentation on these fabrics consisted primarily of stripes and geometric shapes, noted for their indistinct, fuzzy outlines. This technique in Central Asia is called "abrbandi", and the fabrics "abr".

Such a different dolls
Anastacia Lee

CONTENT

Publisher
Marat Akhmedjanov
publisher@ocamagazine.com

Co-Publisher
Aleksandra Vlasova
silkroadmedia.copublisher@gmail.com

Representative in Uzbekistan
Guljamal Pirenova
assistant.kg@ocamagazine.com

Representative in Kazakhstan
Anna Suslova
anna@ocamagazine.com

Representative in Kyrgyzstan
Anastasia Noskova
kyrgyzstan@ocamagazine.com

Project manager
Guljamal Pirenova
assistant.kg@ocamagazine.com

Proof reading
Nick Rowan
nick.rowan@ocamagazine.com

Designer
Nick Kim
designer@ocamagazine.com

Authors:
Andrea Leuenberger, Neville McBain, Alvirt
Akhmedjanov, Vladimir Dolgiy, Alexandra
Vlasova, Andrey Kudryashov

Photographers:
Anastacia Lee, Anton Kovalenko, Alexander
Yesipov, Melanie Everett, Mamadaliev
Sunnat, Andrea Leuenberger, Deniza
Chalbash, Zafar Khusanov

Silk Road Media
Suite 125, 43 Bedford street,
Covent Garden, London, WC2E 9HA

Uzbekistan
Tel.: +998 90 189 57 11,
+998 90 930 87 04
www.centralasia.travel

UZBEKISTAN
DISCOVERY
TRAVEL GUIDE

Disclaimer
The information contained in this publication is for general
information purposes only. The information is provided by
Discovery Uzbekistan travel guide and while we endeavour to
ensure the information up to date and correct, we make no
representations or warranties of any kind, express or implied,
about the completeness, accuracy, reliability or suitability
of the information, products, services, or related graphics
represented for any purpose. Any reliance you place on such
information is therefore strictly at your own risk.

All authors provide their own material and any opinions
contained within are solely those of the authors and do not
neccessarily represent the views or opinions of Discovery
Uzbekistan travel guide. We publish these views as part of
our provision of a forum for discussion and readers should be
aware that the views may contrast each other in the pursuit of
this aim. In no event will we be liable for any loss or damage
including without limitation, indirect or consequential loss or
damage, or any loss or damage whatsoever arising from loss
of data or profits arising out of, or in connection with, the use
of material contained within this publication.

Printed by Mega Printing in Turkey